Champagne Girl in a Budweiser Family

A MEMOIR IN STORIES

Suzanne Weerts

Printed in the United States of America
Paperback ISBN: 979-8-9994979-0-1
Ebook ISBN: 979-8-9994979-1-8

To Maddie and Jack, my heart,
my inspiration and my raison d'être.

Contents

Disclaimer

T his is a compilation of tales from a simpler time, a mostly enchanted childhood lived with far fewer external influences than in our modern world. The stories within these pages are mostly true, marginally misremembered, assuredly embellished, and likely somewhat inaccurate—though always sincerely shared and peppered with the music that has become the soundtrack of my life. Some names and distinguishing characteristics are changed to protect identities, avoid embarrassing people, or because my memory is more rooted in the impression they made than the name they had. Others are real and are meant to be a tribute to the meaningful roles these people played in my life. I've relied on memory, which is inevitably fallible, but I hope my recollections inspire readers who grew up in the "olden days" to reflect on our good fortune to have come of age in a time free of devices, and to have survived our vices. Dive in. The water is warm. And the ice cream truck is just around the corner.

Little Suzanne: Mommy, read me a story.
Mom: There's no time for that, but I'll tell you one.

There Was a Little Girl

There was a little girl,
Who had a little curl.
Right in the middle of her forehead.
When she was good,
She was very very good,
But when she was bad she was horrid.
—Henry Wadsworth Longfellow

CHAPTER ONE
Blackberry Stains

Farm Gate Road becomes a dirt road about a half mile up, and about fifty yards beyond that, the dirt road narrows to a scraggly path and we stop. Daddy puts down the kickstand, parks his bike, and unbuckles my little brother from the red plaid metal seat. Mom has stopped her bike behind him, and Dad reaches for me as she kicks at her kickstand with her navy blue Keds. Daddy unbuckles the thin strap that anchors me to the seat, even though I could totally do it myself. I'm six, after all, but I love when he plucks me out of my blue plaid seat and twirls me through the air, over the honeysuckle and blackberry bushes bursting with the scrumptious scents of summer. My pigtails bounce in the breeze. Of course, we're not wearing helmets. They haven't been invented yet.

Daddy and Mom have made buckets from Maxwell House coffee tins with wire coat hangers, and we each grab one off the handlebars and begin filling the cans with blackberries, the dark purple juice dripping down our arms. Mom knew this would happen so she made sure we dressed in our oldest clothes. My shorts have a hole in the crotch that isn't worthy of a patch and my t-shirt is stained with last summer's blackberry fingerprints from hands one year smaller. The smeared sweetness of a summer Saturday gone by.

My brother, Billy, grabs a stick from a ditch and like Artemus Gordon in our favorite show *The Wild Wild West,* he takes on my

James West holding a thorny branch of dead blackberry briar in a friendly duel.

"If you're not careful, you'll poke your eye out!" admonishes our ever-cautious mother as she grabs plump berries from the bursting vines.

Mom looks like Jackie O. Her hair is perfectly coifed in a brunette bouffant, her pale blue shorts coordinate with her blue checkered sleeveless top. She is graceful and refined. There was no berry picking in Brooklyn where she grew up. She likes this part of her children's childhood in the South.

When we're home, Daddy will make his famous flaky piecrusts using a big blob of Crisco, and fill them with berries boiled with sugar. If there is a little leftover crust, he'll make my brother and me each a tiny pie that we can hold in our hands.

But first we have to get there to get our berries in the pot. With our homemade buckets balancing on the handlebars, arms lightly etched with a Morse code of bramble scratches, our parents steer down the rock-pocked path to the pothole-pitted dirt road. Careful not to spill the berries, we bounce in the back, holding on to the metal armrests, barely tethered in by thin plastic belts, squealing with delight with what feels to us like an E-ticket ride, then crying with dismay as fistfuls of our *pickins* plop along the route.

It is less than a mile along the paved streets home to our cul-de-sac, where Mom pulls into the driveway and Daddy, inexplicably, parks his bike along the curb, pulling the buckets off the handlebars and forgetting his other precious cargo, my brother. Perhaps he thought the bike was sturdier than it was, leaning against a foot-long kickstand, propped along the curb. Perhaps he was contemplating the pies he was about to bake. I am already in the house, ready for the required tick-check and bath before I get to stand on a kitchen chair and stir the pot of fruit and sugar. I am in the entry hall when the screen door slams behind me and I hear Mom scream and I see her running across the expanse of our front lawn, which is only twenty yards, but memory makes it two hundred and it all feels like slow motion. And Daddy is standing in the middle of the grass, immobile with pails of berries in his hands, and he is looking at her quizzically while beyond him is a toppled bike and a little boy upside down, crumpled on a cement curb like a rag doll, not moving.

I step onto the porch, holding open the door because things are speeding up now and my mother is crossing the yard with my brother in her arms and yelling, "How could you be so stupid?" and Daddy is explaining how he was heading right back after he put down the berries, and then Mom is down on the rug in the den cradling my baby brother with blackberry juice stains looking a lot like blood on his t-shirt, and Daddy puts the buckets on the counter then reaches for the phone. He isn't fast enough, I guess, because Mom is already making the call and stretching the extra-long curlicue phone cord into the kitchen where she is rummaging through the freezer, eventually dumping a tray of ice into a dishtowel and talking to 911, describing the baseball-size knot on my baby brother's head, now hidden by the mustard-yellow towel. And my brother still hasn't moved. He looks like Victoria, the Madame Alexander doll grandma bought me at Cameron Village, but Victoria cries when you turn her over and Billy hasn't made a sound. He hasn't moved a bit.

Now maybe all that took five minutes. Maybe it was thirty. At some point in time, while my mother is talking to the doctor, my brother twitches. He squirms. He gingerly sits up. Mom is cradling her baby over one shoulder with the phone in the crook of the other.

"He'll be four in a few weeks," I hear her say. "Ok. Ok. Well, we'll bring him in shortly."

She absentmindedly hands my father the receiver and shares what she gleaned from the call mixed with what she remembers about concussions from nursing school. The wet towel and a few pieces of ice sit soaking into the rug.

Eventually, the bump on my brother's head goes down. There may have been stitches, maybe there was an MRI. My brother has no recollection of what happened to him, but the incident doesn't go unremembered.

Every time Billy came home with a behavioral note on his report card or a less-than-stellar grade in elementary school, "Well, if he hadn't hit his head when he was three, surely things would be different," my mother would say.

If he'd get moody or belligerent as a preteen, "Had he not fallen off that bicycle..." Mom would admonish my father.

If he'd strike out in baseball or miss a critical shot in a basketball game and my dad would express frustration, Mom would purse her lips and shake her head, eyes narrowly aimed in accusation at my dad as if to say, "He'd be a star player if only you'd not ruined his chances."

When they were called to the principal's office when my brother was in high school, Mom just knew it was Dad's fault.

And when my brother became a poet and musician and grew his hair long in college and my father threatened to sneak into his room at night with scissors to chop it all off during Christmas break, Mom sat on the couch in righteous recollection of that afternoon in 1971, when the sun was out and the blackberries were ripe and the pies had to wait because my brother was limp on the floor and lucky because, really, in the end he was fine. But for my mother, it was a stain on my dad's parenting record that she could never get out.

CHAPTER TWO
Hansel and Gretel

I don't remember what she did that made us so mad, but my brother and I retreated to my bedroom and plotted our escape. Maybe she'd run out of Velveeta and insisted we eat our broccoli with no cheese. Maybe she'd made us turn off *The Brady Bunch* and demanded we rake the leaves and pine straw that covered the hill on the side of our house. Maybe she'd hung our underpants on the clothesline again even though we'd begged her not to because all the neighbor kids could see them when we played baseball in the Kenneys' backyard. Whatever it was, we were fed up with being treated like second-class citizens and having our concerns and happiness disregarded.

She never understood how important *The Andy Griffith Show* was to us and would saunter into the den and turn off the television set and say things like, "You kids need to get outside or find something useful to do around the house." Why couldn't she be gentle like Aunt Bee, Wilma Flintstone or Carol Brady? Why couldn't we have Alice looking after us, and making decent meals like the Bradys?

There we were in my room with its four-poster bed covered in the strawberry quilt hand-stitched by Grandma Rose, filling my pink and white-checkered pillowcase with all the necessities we would need in the Big Wide World. Mr. Duck and Theodore Edward Bear, fuzzy slippers and long-sleeved shirts, a paperback copy of *Harriet The Spy* and a diary with a lock.

Billy went to his room and filled his pillowcase with Curious George, Hot Wheels, Underoos and his Redskins jacket, and we snuck down the stairs to grab supplies from the pantry. A couple cans of SpaghettiOs, two tubes of Ritz crackers, a jar of Tang and the bag of Cheerios straight out of the box. She'd never know they were gone if the box was still there. The Cheerios would come in handy, like a trail of breadcrumbs, so that we could find our way back should we ever choose to return.

Mom was a Wicked Witch and we had to get out of there. At six and eight-years-old, we were Hansel and Gretel, and we needed to get home to our real mom. Our Brady Bunch mom.

As we quietly threw our sacks over our shoulders and gently closed the screen door, we heard her say, "Children, want me to bake you some cookies?"

Oh, we knew why she really was turning on the oven.

We snuck down the driveway, dodging behind three seasons of living Christmas trees, and made our way through the dogwoods and sweetgums casting spooky shadows across the sidewalk. I suggested we follow the North Star like the Wise Men, though we knew nothing of the skies, so we were likely following Pluto, which was still considered a planet back then. Where could we go that was north? New York? Canada? Our grandparents lived in Capitol Towers old folks' home in North Raleigh. It would be a long walk, but at least Grandma was liberal with bowls of M&Ms and she never made us do chores.

Billy was dutifully dropping Cheerios, but he ran out before we got to the main street, where only an occasional car whizzed by in a blinding flash of headlights and the sidewalks ended.

"Which way to Grandma's?" I asked the darkness. My little brother wouldn't know, and the North Star or Pluto was no real guide. As an explorer or runaway, I was way out of my league. I should have plotted this whole thing out a little better before we set off. I made an executive decision. Likely my first. *I think we should turn back.* Like Gilligan to my Skipper, Billy followed me, Cheerios crunching under our feet. As we snuck back into the house, the smell of cookies greeted us, our mother never knowing that her runaways had run away and returned.

CHAPTER THREE
A Star is Born

As soon as my first-grade teacher told us there was going to be a talent show, there was little doubt in my mind that I would have a starring role. Contained within my earliest memories was the certainty that I had talent.

"You are a born artist," my grandmother exclaimed when I presented her with a tempera paint interpretation of a lopsided square blue house with a red triangle roof and orange parallelogram windows.

"You could be a prima ballerina one day," said my mother as I twirled around the den until I fell into the ottoman, dizzy and as yet unaware of the practice of spotting.

Clearly, my voice was also exceptional. After all, I was given a solo at kindergarten graduation and was well on my way to being a renowned singer-songwriter as my piece was an original. "Thank You God For Everything" was sung to the tune of "Twinkle, Twinkle Little Star," otherwise known as "The ABC Song." My chart-topping hit of 1971 concluded with a request for forgiveness when we're bad, which likely warmed the hearts of the parents in the pews at Westminster Presbyterian church as I held my hands in prayer under my construction-paper mortarboard. Certainly, it was plain to see they had witnessed the profound piety of a prodigy. My parents beamed at the church hall reception as they nibbled their oatmeal cookies and sipped sherbet punch.

So when Mrs. Aiken told the class about the upcoming talent show, my mind began swirling with possibilities. I could break out my baton or my hula hoop! I'd mastered an impressive driveway dance atop my Hasbro Romper Stompers, kind of a prequel to the Broadway hit *Stomp*, only two decades too early.

Ah, but I had my new red ballet costume from my first recital. Simple satin and tulle with a row of silver sequins across the chest, it was my favorite piece of clothing. Obviously, my classmates at Henry Adams Elementary deserved the opportunity to see me sparkling in cinnamon-spice magnificence in the multipurpose room with its curtained-off stage that was filled with playground equipment when not used for performances. Those curtains held the stale scents of a dozen years of meatloaf and fish sticks from the adjacent cafeteria kitchen.

I immediately went to work on my choreography, choosing the most balletic album in my parents' record collection, *The Nutcracker Suite*. I decided my song would be "The Spanish Dance." It was less than two minutes long and I was able to incorporate all the relevés, sautés and battement tendus that I'd learned in my seven months of intensive, once-a-week, half-hour ballet lessons.

My heart was pounding at the audition as I handed the assistant principal my album and told him the song I'd be dancing to. I arabesqued my little heart out and secured a spot in the lineup, further confirming, in my mind, that I was clearly gifted at my craft, though there is a good chance that anyone who wanted to perform made the cast.

On the evening of the talent show, the multipurpose room echoed with folding chairs squeaking on the linoleum and voices of parents, grandparents, classmates and much, much older kids with feet twice the size of mine in my tiny pink ballet slippers. I hadn't thought about who would be watching me. I'd never considered that an audience might not love my every move.

I was peeking out from between the dusty green curtains to get an idea of where my parents were sitting when I saw him: the neighborhood bully, Ritchie Brown, who had chosen a front-row seat next to a group of other giant fourth graders, clearly ready to heckle the heck out of anyone daring enough to take the stage. I adjusted my routine in my head, plotting how I might spend more time dancing upstage and away from his grimacing, puffed pink face.

My heart pounded as I stood backstage waiting for the first castanet clicks of Tchaikovsky's Spanish "Hot Chocolate" dance, and when the music started, I tippytoed across the back of the stage, then twirled in an unruly ruckus of ruby tulle for the full two minutes. But the music didn't stop. Whoever was in charge of the record must have gotten distracted so I persisted in pirouetting. As long as there was music, I figured the show must go on. And on. And on.

I briefly forgot my intention to avoid spending any time downstage and spun toward the audience, where Ritchie and his friends shouted, "Boo! You can't dance!" and "Get off the stage!"

A lump caught in my throat as I petit jetéd my way back to my comfort zone. I turned up my smile to mask the tears tickling my eyelashes.

I hadn't choreographed the next steps, so I used every dance move I could think of, arabesquing through the nearly four minutes of the Arabian Dance, then chasséing through the minute-long Chinese dance, and then I spent another minute rond de jambing in Russia. I was rotating through the Reed Pipes when the audio person must have realized that the six-year-old on stage had been repeating her repertoire for eight full minutes at this point. The album finally scratched to indicate the end of my performance. Out of breath, I curtsied to polite and likely relieved applause, then tiptoed off the stage, knowing that when I saw my parents, I'd get a good review.

CHAPTER FOUR

Santa Baby

s I pore through the Sears catalog on the braided rug in the den, the light of the Christmas tree reflects off the glossy pages as I dog-ear my dreams. I have great hopes that this year will be different. Surely Santa will recognize my unequivocal *need* for an Easy Bake Oven and Baby Alive, the doll that can eat and pee. My list is long but my belief is large. It is absolutely clear to me that Santa is the real deal because there is no way my parents would have given me a bicycle last year. Then again, Santa got Lynn a bike *and* an oven *and* the Barbie Dream House.

"It's because Lynn is an only child," Mom said. "She needs more toys because she doesn't have a brother."

I look over at mine, wearing that stupid cowboy hat he never takes off and a cap gun in his holster as he adds marbles to a Barrel of Monkeys, then shakes them incessantly just to annoy me. I'd rather have the Easy Bake Oven.

When Christmas finally comes and we bound down the stairs to check out our loot, inevitably I am disappointed. Santa always seems to pay attention to the bottom of my list: the stuffed animal, the book, the Pet Rock. But what about all the important things I starred at the top of the page? Does Santa need glasses?

And *something* is suspicious. I am seven and I'm not stupid. I wrote a letter to Santa reminding him of what we discussed at the mall. The oven is critically important to my happiness and it would be best if it comes with a bunch of cake mixes because I know Mom won't readily buy me more. But when I dump out my stocking, where obviously the little boxes of mixes should be, there is a View-Master and reels like *The Seven Wonders of the World* and *America's National Parks*. That wasn't on my list at all. And there is a message from Santa: *Sorry, but we ran out of ovens this year.* What? Ran out of ovens! You're Santa! You can make more. But then I notice something. Santa's writing is slanted way to the left in a familiar sort of way. It kind of resembles the note I brought to school when I was sick last month. It looks just like my father's writing.

So I confront him. "Daddy, did you write this note from Santa?"

And my father does not say, "Well, Santa was so busy, he asked me to let you know about the Easy Bake shortage." I so love the magic of Christmas that I would believe him. But like George Washington and the cherry tree, my father cannot tell a lie. He calls over my brother, who is only five, and sits us both on his lap and reveals the truth about the North Pole and the elves, the sled and the toys, all the stories from the books and holiday films that we've had only a few years to revel in. I am crushed by the sad reality, but more so for my brother, because I could have kept this secret for several more years and given him a longer childhood. I actually would have loved to be the only kid in my house who was in the know! What the heck?

But it does at least explain why no oven and the crappy View-Master. My parents are cheapskates. I overhear my mother whisper-yelling at my dad, "Why did you tell them?" She's clearly angry, but not as much as I am. I didn't set out to figure this out. I wanted the magic to last. I liked having hope that something could surprise me. Instead, I sit on the braided rug with my View-Master, losing myself in the images of distant lands. San Francisco, Egypt, the Grand Tetons. I want to see all these places. I want to see anything but this faded braided rug and the boxes filled with empty promises.

CHAPTER FIVE
Backyard Olympics

I t was the summer of 1976. The red, white and blue "Freedom Train" had just rolled through Raleigh, North Carolina, stopping on the tracks across from the State Fairgrounds. Everyone I knew, from my teachers and friends at Henry Adams Elementary school to the checkout lady at Piggly Wiggly, lined up to see George Washington's copy of the United States Constitution, the original Louisiana Purchase agreement, and Judy Garland's dress from *The Wizard of Oz.* There were replicas of Jesse Owens' 1936 gold medals and a real-life rock from the moon in this rolling museum that celebrated America's bicentennial.

A wave of patriotism had swept across the country. The stars and stripes were proudly displayed off the porch posts of just about every house on my block. My friends and I marched around our subdivision dressed as "The Spirit of 76," encouraging neighbors to sign up for the 4th of July potluck we were organizing in our cul-de-sac.

A week later, we gathered in my den as Queen Elizabeth proclaimed the opening of Montreal's Olympic Games. Sweating with Olympic fever in our un-air-conditioned house, we decided to host our own Olympics.

The backyard smelled of fresh-cut grass and honeysuckle as the lightning bugs began their summer evening dance and our planning committee put the final touches on the medals and the schedule of events. All the neighborhood kids had agreed to be in at least one competition and serve as the fans in the lawn chair stands for the rest. The games were to be staged in the Pyechas' backyard because they had a wooden balance beam and chin-up bar in the cluster of pine trees behind their house, as well as an ample patch of grass between those trees and the patio to allow for the 50-yard dash and a number of other key events.

The shiny insides of Peter Pan peanut butter jar lids became our gold medals, threaded with the stretchy golden ribbon from my mother's Christmas bows and tags box. We covered Smucker's and Hellmann's lids with tinfoil to make the silver medals. Bronze recipients were to receive brown construction paper circles with BRONZE written on them in black crayon.

On the day of the big event, Tommy Kenney brought over his Socker Boppers so we could reenact the gold medal-winning maneuvers of Sugar Ray Leonard and Leon Spinks. Back when Bruce Jenner had no connection to the Kardashians and seemed unquestionably masculine, we were in awe of his athleticism. We recreated many of the Decathlon events that earned him the title of "World's Greatest Athlete," throwing Mrs. Pyecha's broomstick for the javelin, a baking potato for the shot-put, and using the bright yellow melamine dishes that came as gifts with purchases of Purina Dog Chow as our discuses.

Beth Sanders was the tallest among the neighbor kids at the time and she beat out all the boys in the long jump, with a Hayloft Circle record 8.9 feet, measured with yardsticks from Mrs. Lucas' sewing closet. We tried to pole-vault with the broomstick javelin, but it was a bust. It was too hot and muggy to run all the way around the block, so we rode our bikes instead. Patrick Kenney probably wouldn't have won the gold if some of us hadn't stopped at Lynn Richman's house on Rail Fence Road for a Fudgsicle midway through the ride.

But the highlight of the Backyard Olympics was the gymnastics competition. Nadia Comaneci was only fourteen, just a few years older than most of us. She scored seven perfect 10s and we were all sure that we, too, had what it took to be gold-medal winners one day. Granted, none of us had ever taken a gymnastics class and only Lynn Lucas had a decent roundoff to speak of. The rest of us were limited to imperfect cartwheels and somersaults, but that didn't stop us from attempting to duplicate the moves of Nellie Kim and Olga Korbut.

We had three events in our competition: the balance beam, the bar, and the floor exercise. A couple of forward rolls were attempted on the beam, but mostly the challenge was simply staying on it, jumping and turning and adding arm flourishes before attempting to stick a landing in a mulchy cushion of pine straw and leaves.

The bar was a 1½-inch metal pipe anchored between two splintering 2x4s about six feet off the ground. Pull-ups and chin-ups earned points in our competition, as did hanging by the knees and not touching the ground. Paul Kenney took home the gold by completing a flipping dismount and nearly sticking his landing before he toppled into the pine straw.

The final event of the Backyard Olympics of '76 was the floor exercise. The girls in the neighborhood worked hard on that one. None of the boys wanted to compete so they agreed to be judges. We chose our music and honed our top-secret moves in the privacy of our own living rooms in preparation for the big event. I covertly carried my parents' album, *The Hits of '66*, up to the Pyechas' house in a Holly Hobbie pillowcase. No way was I going to give away any part of my highly competitive routine.

Beth went first. Her cartwheels were clean, her choreography tight to Leo Sayer's "You Make Me Feel Like Dancing," her

Endless Flight album spinning on my brother's Mickey Mouse turntable on the back patio. Lynn was up next, showing off high kicks peppered with a number of her signature roundoffs to KC and The Sunshine Band's "Shake Your Booty." Audra Pyecha, wearing her red, white and blue-striped swimsuit, then pulled out her *Wild Cherry* record and performed a dizzying series of forward rolls for over three minutes to "Play That Funky Music." Rising from the ground with the world still spinning and her back covered in grass, she fell over a couple times before she made it to the mesh lawn chair to await her scores.

Meanwhile I carefully snuck my music onto the record player, setting the needle on "These Boots Are Made for Walkin,'" just as Mrs. Pyecha called from the kitchen window, "Anyone want some Kool-Aid?"

We all rushed inside for Twinkies and strawberry punch. Just the energy I would need to achieve the gold medal, I thought. But when we went outside, my dreams were destroyed. *The Hits of '66* had melted on the turntable.

How could I perform my brilliantly choreographed dance and cartwheel combos with no music? I was forced to borrow Lynn's record and adapt my moves to "I'm Your Boogie Man," and I am quite sure that is why I went home with the brown-paper bronze.

CHAPTER SIX
Pet Cemetery

I was six when I went to my first funeral. It was a palpable heartbreak. Goldie had come into my life at the Henry Adams Elementary Family Festival in an air and water-filled plastic bag after I successfully cast my plastic rod over the blue sheet hanging in the doorway to Mrs. Aycock's fifth grade class's GO FISH booth.

Goldie was the first pet I'd ever had that was *all mine.* I spent hours listening to Danny Kaye reading *Grimm's Fairy Tales* on my Mickey Mouse turntable as Briar Rose, Rumpelstiltskin and Clever Gretel faced their challenges on the crackling recording. These were dark stories of strangers and real dangers, the consequences of greed and the power of love. I took it all in while staring into the fishbowl on my dresser, and of course I melodramatically related to the clever servant girl outwitting her master as I plotted how I, too, might get out of the miserable chore of setting the table. Goldie stared back, her round lips opening and closing, telling me everything was ok.

And Goldie was right, until she wasn't. I came home from school one afternoon, about six weeks after she joined my bedside menagerie of a dozen stuffed animals and one once-living fish, and there she was, floating belly-up in her bowl. I was devastated, especially when I learned of my father's plan to flush Goldie down the toilet. I myself was flushed from several hours of sobbing when I talked my mother into helping me give Goldie a proper burial.

We put her in a Russell Stover's sampler box and found a spot between the shed and the garden. I carefully buried the box under a lasagna of dirt, kitchen mulch and pine needles. My family gathered around as I stuck a popsicle stick cross with the crayon tribute *Best Fish Ever* into Goldie's resting spot and I spoke of Goldie's kindness and her importance in my life while my little brother, required to wear his Sunday best, drove his Matchbox car up Daddy's leg.

"Goldie was loved by everyone who met her," I declared as I flashed back to the two friends who'd visited since Goldie joined the family, and the slightly interested glances they cast in her direction en route to my basket of Barbies.

Then we all retreated to the house for a refreshing glass of bright orange Tang and Pepperidge Farm Goldfish crackers in Goldie's honor, which might sound a bit morbid considering we'd just buried her, but I thought it was a fitting tribute.

More fish with popsicle-stick markers would join the Goldie Graveyard over the next few years, and I mourned each passing with poignantly expressed agony, hosting more and more elaborate services with increasingly lengthy eulogies and more extravagant receptions, enlisting my mother's baking and encouraging my dad to fire up the grill for funerary feasts. Finally, Mom declared there would be no more pet fish adopted in our household.

That Easter we got a rabbit. Fuzzy and white with silky pink ears and bright pink eyes. We couldn't believe the Easter Bunny gave us one of his brethren as our new pet hopped around the living room, leaving a trail of tiny round poop balls on Mom's Karastan rug. My brother and I were instantly in love, but as soon as we set about naming him, the battle was on. Our love was for our bunny and not each other. We just couldn't agree

on anything. With his little nose crinkling like Samantha in
Bewitched, "Sniffy" seemed the obvious choice to me. But he was
peeking around a chair leg when my brother declared his name
should be "Peeky." Stupid, I know. We argued for hours before
my mother stepped into the living room ring to call a truce, and
Sniffy-Peeky became her name, kind of the Olivia Newton-John
of hyphenated rabbit names.

Oh, how I loved Sniffy-Peeky! As soon as I got home from
school, I'd rush out to the two-story rabbit hutch that our father
built in the backyard to hold his soft body in my arms. He was
a fast hopper and often escaped my watchful eye, hiding under
the back porch until my father got home and used a rake to
prompt him out from under the Army green metal rowboat.
Neighbors would bring over salad scraps for Sniffy-Peeky to
eat and, like his personal waitress, I'd dump carrot tops and
romaine hearts onto the dining room floor of his hutch.

A pet rabbit can live for eight to twelve years. The lifespan
of cognizant childhood is far shorter. It wasn't long before I got
caught up in teenage extracurriculars and boys and I lost interest in Sniffy-Peeky.

One afternoon, Mrs. Lucas came over with a baggie of greens
for our bunny. "Knock knock!" she announced through the
screen door.

I met her in the entry hall, calling for my mother, who came
around the corner from the kitchen wiping her hands on her
apron as her friend handed over the baggie.

"Oh Joy, Sniffy-Peeky is no longer with us."

"Dottie, I'm so sorry."

"What?!" I cried, with tears instantly tumbling down my
cheeks. "But I love Sniffy-Peeky!" I fell to the floor sobbing; after
all, I'd lost my best friend. "How could this have happened?" I
wailed, looking to my mother for comfort.

"You obviously didn't love him that much," said Mom, a little too matter-of-factly. "He died three months ago and we were wondering how long it would take you to notice." Then she called to my father in the den, "Hey Bill, guess who just realized her rabbit died?"

Dad joined us in the entry hall and the three adults stood there laughing as I lay crumpled on the floor, devastated not just at the loss of my little friend and the flood of guilt I felt for ignoring him but also that I'd become a joke to my parents. And I'd been ripped off on giving him a proper funeral.

"Where is he buried?" I whimpered.

"He's in your goldfish graveyard," Mom said.

I immediately got to work on his marker. The solo service was my own private penance, the empty hutch serving as a constant reminder.

CHAPTER SEVEN

Easy A

There's a land that I see where the children are free
And I say it ain't far to this land from where we are
Take my hand, come with me, where the children are free
Come with me, take my hand, and we'll live
In a land where the river runs free
In a land through the green country
In a land to a shining sea
And you and me are free to be you and me
—The New Seekers, "Free to Be…You and Me"

"Stop the crying bit or I'll give you something to cry about!" Daddy yelled as I sat pink-faced at the dinner table, lima bean mush sitting in my throat like a hairball in the sink drain, which also often earned paternal outbursts. Chances are I'd just dropped my napkin or leaned back in my chair with the frame creaking precariously close to the sliding glass door, which I was now wishing I could fall through like Alice's Looking Glass.

On *Free to Be…You and Me*, football player Rosey Grier appeared much bigger than my dad and sang "It's Alright to Cry," but clearly my father didn't buy into any of those Hollywood shenanigans. I sided with Rosey, and tears became my best form of self-expression in the face of my father's regular rants. I was an open-faced sandwich of emotions at the dinner table. But I could easily lose myself in the words of Marlo Thomas and friends singing about a land where the children are free, dreaming of a place where I'd not be saddled with stupid chores, guilt trips, and angry outbursts, and would most definitely be free from homework.

I'd been assigned yet another stupid report. This one was on reptiles. And I was going to need to get my request in fast, otherwise someone else would get to do the alligator and I'd be stuck with the adder.

All my life, I'd longed to own a set of World Book Encyclopedias so I wouldn't have to beg my mother to drive me to the local library whenever I was assigned a school report. I imagined the ease of doing research in my very own home. Over the years, encyclopedia salesmen, in their felt fedoras and suspenders, came calling at our house. I'd listen in on the conversation between the screen door as my mother kindly said, "We'll think about it," knowing full well that meant NO.

"Why have something that takes up so much space and costs so much money when you can borrow it for free?" was Mom's supposedly logical response.

But the encyclopedia salesmen all did something that forever changed the trajectory of my academic knowledge. So that my mother had something to ponder and peruse, they each gave her the "A" volume to try out. "No obligation to buy and you can keep it even if you determine you don't want the rest," they'd tell her.

That is how my family came to own the "A" *Encyclopedia Brittanica*, *Funk & Wagnall's Volumes 1* and *2*, both *Colliers* and *Compton's Books* "A," and the "A" *World Book Encyclopedia*, which meant that when my fourth-grade teacher assigned animal reports, I did mine on the aardvark. When my seventh-grade teacher's fall project was countries of the world, I chose Argentina. Throughout my childhood I did reports on the Amazon, Arizona, Agamemnon, Abigail Adams, Arches National Park, Jane Austen, Argon, Louis Armstrong and Attila the Hun. It was a different version of getting straight As in school.

Those encyclopedias always got me started in my attempt at the quickest report. I preferred to spend my time on its presentation, drawing and coloring the most elaborate cover sheets and designing unique visual aids out of things I found around the house. There were no Michael's or Hobby Lobby stores back then so we had to use whatever we could find in junk drawers or in the yard to devise our dioramas. I could frequently be found on the den floor surrounded by a stack of popsicle sticks, bottle caps, fabric scraps and rubber cement that my brother would roll into balls pretending they were boogers as he fake-sneezed them into my hair and onto the ottoman.

All the while I just longed to be free to venture into the Bs or—even wilder—something exotic in maybe the Ms or the Rs. Oh, the possibilities of a life lived outside the box—or at least outside the confines of the letter A!

CHAPTER EIGHT

The Acorn Assassin

W hen I was eleven, I almost killed all of the children in my neighborhood. My flirtation with potential mass murder began innocently enough. It was the summer of 1977. Long, sweaty days of playing Red Rover and King of the Mountain blended into nights spent waiting for the ice cream truck to come jangling down Old Farm Road to the base of our cul-de-sac, where we'd shell out fifty cents of hard-earned allowance for orange Push-Ups and ice cream sandwiches and sit on the curb licking drips off our wrists. I loved my friends. I didn't set out to kill them.

But the Indian village was my idea. We were bored and needed to come up with a way to make money to support our ice cream truck and Wacky Packages habit. Remember those? Sticker packs of popular products with colorful, goofy graphics and punny names like *Unlucky Charms* cereal, *Cup of Poodles*, and *Durahell* batteries? We had to have more and more to cover our Slam Books and school folders. It was an addiction.

Dad built us a teepee with long branches from the sweetgum tree and two-by-fours left over from constructing his shed. We covered it in my brother's old red and blue plaid bedspread and inside, our Girl's Club met in a circle on the grass with a Tupperware bowl full of homemade Chex Mix to plot our money-making scheme.

We planned to sell the kind of things I'd seen at the Oconaluftee Village in Cherokee, North Carolina. We'd offer war paint for a nickel using the mini tubes of Avon lipstick samples. We set out to make a dozen clay pots out of the bountiful mud under the back porch. The musky red clay felt cool and smooth in our hands as we shaped it into bowls the size of baseballs and let them dry in the sun on the driveway after we pressed beads and seashells into them, as surely the Indians would have done.

My mother had taken up macrame several years before, so we dug through her long-since abandoned supplies and finished off a dozen beaded bracelets. We spent a week weaving colorful potholders on our square metal looms, and we encouraged our parents to serve corn on the cob, then used the husks to make cornhusk dolls with raffia belts, corn silk hair and permanent marker smiles. We collected a basket of acorns and used the tops as cups and bowls for our doll display.

That's when I had the bright idea to make authentic Indian food. Surely the hunter/gatherer Indians of the Southern Piedmont – the Lumbee, Catawba and Cherokee – would have made use of the pile of acorns minus their cupule caps lying in the crabgrass in my front yard. I cracked them open and pulled out clumps of the creamy yellow flesh and proceeded to mash them into a gooey paste. It tasted sour and acidic. I could fix that. I added a quarter cup of sugar and a half cup of milk, creating a grits-like mixture that wasn't too terrible. We made a sign, selling Dixie mouthwash cups of "Real Indian Food" for ten cents.

Flyers featuring crayon drawings of our teepee advertised the grand opening of The Old Farm Indian Village. A Girl's Club member was stationed at the end of the driveway in a lawn chair with our shoebox cash register on a TV tray ready to accept the nickel admission price. We went cheap with the admission charge in hope that people would be more inclined to spring for the fifty cents to a dollar that we were asking for the clay pots, potholders, bracelets and cornhusk dolls.

It was clear that none of the lipstick-war paint-covered boys in the neighborhood were going to buy any of our wares as they did war dances around our wigwam. Our mothers purchased most of them out of sympathy, guilt, or perhaps appreciation for our efforts. I'm pretty sure a couple moms made two-for-one bargains or bartered for high-value snacks for the starving native craftswomen, like Ho Hos or Twinkies.

It wasn't until the mothers left that I realized I'd forgotten my *pièce de résistance* and went in the house to get the tray of single-serving size acorn mush cups out of the fridge. We had about fifteen kids standing in my yard daring one another to eat the authentic Indian food when Mrs. Lucas came over to purchase another potholder.

She asked what we were doing and got all concerned. She rushed to my front door and told my mother, a registered nurse, who got on the phone with Mrs. Kenney, also a nurse, who rushed over with a small bottle of syrup of ipecac as they hurriedly pulled old nursing schoolbooks and those A encyclopedias off the shelves in the den while Mrs. Lucas called poison control. Suddenly all hell broke loose.

We kids stood in the grass by the teepee, trying to determine if the nausea we might have been feeling was due to being poisoned or if it was psychosomatic. My brother was moaning and clutching his stomach, turning in circles in a mock death dance designed to make me feel as guilty as possible. Was it me or did Audra look ashen?

Apparently large amounts of ingested acorns *can* induce severe illness and the tannic and gallic acids *can* cause damage to the gastrointestinal system and kidneys. That was the information gleaned from a medical book, but Mrs. Lucas was still on the line with poison control. I could see her stretching the phone cord toward the bay window as she assessed our condition. Mrs. Kenney was standing by with the ipecac and a spoon.

In the dappled light coming through the sycamore tree, Beth definitely had taken on a yellow glow. Kidney failure leads to jaundice and jaundice made a person look yellow. I knew that from mom's stories of my birth. And an early blood transfusion. My brother let out a melodramatic moan and Paul Kenney joined in, collapsing to the grass and writhing in fake pain. Mrs. Kenney rushed toward him with her spoon just as Mrs. Lucas came out of the house, the screen door slamming behind her. She assured us that we'd all live, prescribing applesauce to calm any troubled tummies. Mom gave each of her friends a jar of Motts from the pantry, apologizing profusely for my overzealous behavior. *Overzealous!* She used that word often to describe me.

My zeal returned as I remembered our cash box and I got excited over the thought of counting our earnings, hoping we'd not be asked to return the acorn mush money. But when I looked at the card table, the box was gone. We were soon engrossed in a new *Charlie's Angels* caper, during which it was deduced that the neighborhood bully, Ritchie Brown, had been skulking near the end of the driveway during the poison control commotion. No one would risk joining me in knocking on his door and demanding what was rightfully ours, and I didn't dare go alone. Ritchie's dad was known for sitting on his front porch and yelling insults at neighbors, often with his shotgun by his side.

For weeks I dreamt up Indian raids on the Brown's house. And when the ice cream truck stopped down the street where Ritchie lived, it pained me to imagine him converting our hard-earned cornhusk cash into a Creamsicle for himself.

CHAPTER NINE
Sandcastles and Reclaimed Kickboards

"**O**h honey, you have champagne tastes, but you're growing up in a Budweiser family," my mom said as I sat at the kitchen table telling her all the places I hoped to travel to one day. Mom filled her electric skillet with a week's worth of leftover vegetables and covered them with a jar of tomato sauce to make her specialty, "Vegetables Italiano." My brother and I groaned as we set the table and smelled the familiar Ragu scent.

"One day you'll understand that these things cost money and you'll learn to be grateful for what you have."

Mom was an expert at using every last thing in her fridge and at lowering expectations. Occasionally, when no lima beans were involved, Vegetables Italiano tasted surprisingly good.

Growing up in our split-level house, I just assumed everyone's mother used a razor blade to cut open the fully squeezed-out toothpaste tube, scraping our brushes with the last remnants. I supposed that, when making hamburgers, all moms sliced the patties through the center to make thin circles of *meatishness*. I figured the heart of a good burger meal was the bun since there was always more bread with our burgers than anything else. I thought it normal to add powdered milk to the near-empty jugs dropped off twice monthly by the State Farm milkman so as to avoid the hassles of weekly delivery. It didn't dawn on me that money was tight. Surely everyone made snow boots by putting Wonder Bread bags over socks in their sneakers?

Despite our lack of funds, my parents ensured we went on vacations every summer; granted, we sometimes camped at Atlantic Beach in the back of my dad's Ford pickup truck. My parents and I would squeeze together on top of my brother Billy's twin mattress while Billy attempted to sleep stretched out across the front seat, the sound of Dad's snoring echoing through the Salter Path campground like a jackhammer while acorns dropped on the metal camper shell throughout the night, spurring dreams of Civil War battles long since fought and lost.

Indeed, the Civil War was the backdrop for numerous family road trips. My parents felt it was their duty to educate us about American history and for some reason they zeroed in on the War Between the States.

Because my father had served in the Navy, I was born in a military hospital in Charleston, South Carolina. Two years later, when Dad was stationed in Groton, Connecticut, my brother was born. It was an unfortunate turn of events for me, having a northerner for a brother, because Billy became a battle aficionado during those trips to Civil War battlefields and as a northerner, *he* was on team Ulysses S. Grant. This left me, a southerner by birth, on the side of Robert E. Lee and team Jefferson Davis. While "my people" had a few key victories and I delighted in reading the plaques at Fort Sumter and Manassas, it became clear early on that I was doomed. When it initially seemed that I'd seized Fort Macon in 1861, we soon discovered a sign by a cannon revealing my team lost it to Union forces the following year. Yet another victory for my evil brother and his blue battalion.

Billy had a set of toy soldiers and cannons that he'd line up on picnic tables at our campsites or on the brown and orange floral-print bedspreads of our Howard Johnson's motel rooms. Confederate soldiers tumbled to their doom in Vicksburg, Gettysburg and Port Royal. The fate of slavery did not play a part in our childhood discussions. It wasn't my fault that I was born on the wrong side of the Mason-Dixon line, but my brother regularly made it clear: I was born a loser.

However, it's those childhood travels away from the battlefields that hold a gentler space in my memory, especially when we found ourselves on Emerald Isle, North Carolina.

We'd make the three-hour drive in our Carolina-blue Ford LTD down Highway 58, through quaint towns shaded by trees covered in Spanish moss. As we approached Cape Carteret, the sides of the road would become increasingly sandy and the scent of the ocean filled our lungs. We'd sit on beach towels in the back of the car to keep from sticking to the vinyl seats in the muggy July heat, the car windows open because the air conditioner rarely worked.

The Cameron Langston Bridge over the Intracoastal Waterway arched like a roller coaster over the marshy land, with boats zigging and zagging through the passes, and the island's water tower in the distance resembling a giant golf ball on a tall tee. The first street on the right led straight to the Islander Motel, two stories tall, painted blue and surrounded by unspoiled sand dunes with a sun-bleached wooden walkway leading straight to the beach. This was our paradise.

Daddy would pull up to the registration desk while we bounced in the back seat, anxious to get out of the car, our tushes tired from the long drive during which it had to be an absolute emergency for our father to stop for a bathroom break. If you could hold it, you did, because pain was far better than

Dad's annoyance at pulling off the road at a gas station—or more likely, he'd immediately screech to a halt and offer up a patch of shrubbery in a ditch.

After he got the teal plastic key tag, Daddy would back the car into the parking space right in front of our room. We always opted for the convenience of unloading on the first floor over the view from the second story. And if the room was close to the swimming pool, all the better for us kids.

Bronzed moms in lounge chairs by the pool made the coconut scent of Hawaiian Tropic mixed with cigarettes far more prevalent than the smell of chlorine, likely because there wasn't much. The hotel was blue but the pool was green, the bottom covered in a squishy layer of sand. Clearly, we weren't the only ones dumping the grit out of our bathing suit bottoms after a day at the beach.

My brother and I would rush into the room with its sandy brown shag carpet and we'd jump from bed to bed as our parents unloaded the trunk. We didn't have much actual luggage. Most of our belongings were in brown paper Winn Dixie grocery bags. As soon as the car was unloaded, Daddy would take off to find the local ABC store so he could get the Jim Beam he needed to mix into his Mountain Dew, which undoubtedly enabled him to tolerate a long weekend with his family.

Mom gathered our threadbare towels and her green and white nylon woven metal-framed beach chair and we'd head out on the wood-plank walkway through the seagrass-covered dunes and down the steps to the beckoning Atlantic Ocean.

While our mother dug her feet into the sand and flipped through her *Good Housekeeping* magazine, Billy and I would take off on our own for hours, exploring the dunes as if we were astronauts taking our first steps on the moon or Arabian knights seeking an oasis. It was on one of those adventures—when we were crossing the windswept desert with knots of seagrass standing in as cacti, never planting our feet for more than two seconds at a time on the burning hot sand—that we came upon the broken pieces of a Styrofoam surfboard.

You'd think we found gold in them hills as I stood on the rounded tip, about a foot long, resting my burning feet, and my brother staked his claim to the eighteen-inch middle section. With my smaller discovery, my brother reminded me that I was the loser, but I felt victorious holding my curved chunk of marshmallow-colored heaven. We attempted to surf the sand like Aladdin on magic carpets before taking our new kickboards out to the foaming blue ocean. The joy we got from those rejected pieces of polystyrene lasted for *years*. We carted our kickboards on vacations throughout my childhood and later handed them down to our sisters.

I was ten when one sister was born, and we squeezed her bassinette in the back of Dad's pickup truck between Billy's mattress and the wheel well when we went camping. I was fourteen when my youngest sister came along, and we'd all pile into the new minivan and head to the borrowed basement apartment of one of Dad's work friends a few blocks from the beach, where the cool cement floor and muggy scent of the swamp cooler welcomed us for several summers.

The new additions to our family meant that now whenever we stayed at a motel, my parents made my brother and me hide in the back of the van. They would check in as a family of four, then have us sneak in under cover of darkness, and we'd all cram into the two double beds, my brother often on Dad's old military cot with my youngest sister curled up between the two hotel chairs pushed together, the legs made stationary with Daddy's belt.

Beyond the sunburns and the scent of Solarcaine and mosquito bites dotting my legs, I itched for this time with my family every summer. Daddy on his folding chair with his red NC State stadium cup filled with bourbon-laced Mountain Dew sweating in a pocket of sand by his beach chair, where he'd sit for hours, puffing on his pipe and casting fishing lines toward the tide, occasionally getting a bite. I'd squeal with glee as he reeled in our dinner. Rehousing sand crabs to the castles I'd embossed with limpet, clam and scallop shells and surrounded with a water-filled moat. Splashing in the waves with my brother and our reclaimed kickboards, the sand-dune score of the century. A blessing of a childhood filled with freedom for discovery.

CHAPTER TEN

Itch

I was sitting in the bathtub when I saw it. I'd let the bubbles dissolve until all but a few curled around my toes. The water was cool like dishwater after you'd let the plates soak then forgot about them when you went to the den to watch *Gilligan's Island,* and Mom would yell, "You get back in here and finish your job before you watch television!" just as the Professor was about to try out his new escape plan. There was no such thing as a pause button. You had to wait for the commercial or wait for the rerun.

There, on my stomach, was a single dot. And I knew.

Maybe it was a mosquito bite, I told myself. But further inspection revealed another one inside my elbow and three more on the back of my knee cap. They itched.

"Mom!" I screamed. And within moments she confirmed. It was the chicken pox. Billy had them first and I had done an exceptional job staying away from my brother for weeks. I made him maintain a single cushion on the far end of the couch day after day as we watched afternoon cartoons. I never crossed the pillow line between us. I hadn't sat anywhere near his spot for weeks. I changed chairs at the dinner table to ensure distance. I hunkered down in my room with my books and my Barbies, making certain his door was closed before I'd venture downstairs. I didn't touch the banister. I covered my hand with my shirt before opening the pantry door. I washed my hands so often there wasn't even a little dirt under my fingernails and there was pretty much always dirt under my nails, but not when my brother had the chicken pox.

But Billy had been sick in June and he was mostly better by the 4th of July. I figured I was out of the woods, that my vigilance had paid off. But now the days were heavy with summer heat, and my brother's former agony was my own. Only mine was worse. So much worse.

When it is 96 degrees and humid and your skin itches like it's on fire from the spots between your toes to the insides of your ears and your house has just two window-unit air conditioners that your mother runs only when absolutely necessary, meaning when she is asleep in her own room or cooking adjacent to the window unit over the kitchen sink, what is a nine-year-old covered in pox supposed to do? I tried desperately to scratch the hard-to-reach spots in the center of my back with the turkey fork or by rubbing against tree bark.

Coated in sticky pink calamine lotion, I climbed into the knotty Pawleys Island hammock strung between a couple pine trees and read Charlotte's Web, trying to take my mind off my misery. Sweat beaded on my forehead as rivulets of pale pink calamine trickled down my legs. And I complained. Oh, how I complained. Mom would come out of the house with an icy glass of lemonade, wiping a hand on her apron and sweat off my brow, and I'd moan dramatically, making sure she realized that no one in the history of any illness that was ever suffered had suffered as much as me, itching miserably in that bumpy hammock.

She'd bring out a washcloth hardened in the freezer and put it on the back of my neck.

"Oh, I am definitely dying," I'd whine in a most tragic Scarlett O'Hara voice. After all, tomorrow is just another day—for misery. "If only we had a pool," I lamented. "That would be the only thing that would feel good right now."

Mom went to Kmart the next day and surprised me with a round, blue plastic pool with little fish stamped on the bottom and up the 8-inch sides. She filled it with water from the hose and emptied a tray of ice cubes into it. The ice melted in minutes, but I sat on the back porch somewhat blissful in my tiny pool until it turned into a hot tub, making me itch all the more.

Billy, now smugly carrying immunities to my affliction, was allowed to join me in the pool, and together we filled the space as water spilled over the sides. Every so often Mom would empty a bucket with cool water from the spigot, pouring it over us as we squealed with delight. I briefly forgot my agony until I realized people may no longer be worried about my well-being, at which point I began another tortured moan. Our dog Snoopy, a scrawny white mutt with a handful of spots who tried to pass himself off as a Dalmatian, lapped up pool water until we shooed him away.

Before we got that plastic pool, our swim experience was limited to Howard Johnson's hotel pools and swimming lessons at the NC State Aquatics Center. Occasionally, our neighbors would bring us to the University's Faculty Club. Located in the midst of rolling hills dotted with cows adjacent to the School of Agriculture, it was a luxury to go there, but we always had to be on our best behavior so we could get invited back.

Yet even when we were on our best behavior, Mom always said, "Don't be pests," and we weren't allowed to ask to go. We had to wait for an invitation. So, we'd sit under the dogwood trees on the side of our house, trying our best to look desirable as Mrs. Lucas packed their car with towels and snacks and Lynn climbed into the back.

"Maybe they want some family time," Mom said, and we'd head to our porch, dejected.

Sometimes Mom would set up the rotating sprinkler in the front yard and we'd leap over it until the ground became mushy and our legs were covered in grass.

There was one house in our neighborhood that had a pool. One day, a For Sale sign appeared in that yard at the top of the hill. We begged our parents to buy it, even though it was just one story and probably didn't have as much room as our house. When Mom and Dad declined our sales pitches, we took to hoping, praying, and crossing fingers that the people who did buy it would have a kid our age.

Neighborhood Harriet the Spy that I was, I stalked the real estate agent, eager to assess who might become our new neighbors. When she pulled up at the corner house with the pool in her lime-green Gremlin, I'd ride my bike up and down the street, casually observing her tidying up the front yard in her goldenrod Century 21 jacket, her long brown hair clipped in the back with a tortoiseshell barrette, her fashionable minidress and long, tan, stocking-covered legs. She was the kind of woman my dad would call "a looker" and I couldn't stop looking.

I'd park my bike against the Old Farm sign at the top of the hill and work my way down the block for a better view, my long, lanky shadow dancing in my wake as I darted from Sycamore tree to honeysuckle bush, where I'd strain to hear her discussions with childless couples or people carrying infants. Surely they'd have to be rich if they could afford a $23,000 house. Once a couple with two children showed up. The kids appeared close to our ages. There was hope. I reported back to my brother, and we began plotting how we'd befriend the two before any other kids in the neighborhood stood a chance.

The next day a SOLD sign went on top of the yellow post and our dreams were about to come true. We got our bathing suits ready. But a month later, when the moving truck arrived, there wasn't a kid in sight. The Looker had sold it to a couple without kids. And as far as we could tell, they never even used their pool. What's wrong with some people? You could walk by the tall wood fence on the hottest Saturday in August and there wouldn't be a single splash. What a waste! We knew that just over the fence was a little slice of heaven that we could never reach, like an itch you just couldn't scratch.

CHAPTER ELEVEN
Tomgirl

I was a girly girl. I twirled through the house in gypsy costumes created with scarves draped over my mother's slips and nightgowns, wearing tutus until the tulle was in shreds. I played fairies in my friend Lynn's backyard with the gauzy yellow curtains her mother had replaced from the bay window in their living room.

My alter ego was a tomboy. I climbed trees, built forts, and played football with the neighborhood boys. Paul Kenney once stole one of my Barbies and lit her on fire from his perch in the top of the sweetgum tree, tossing her melting body and flaming hair into a lump of leaves that his brother rushed to put out with a garden hose. In retaliation, I stole his Steve Scout action hero. But instead of warping Steve with lighter fluid, I arranged a marriage between him and my Skipper doll. My brother's Geronimo served as the minister, and the happy couple rode off on Thunderbolt, the plastic horse. Paul would have hated that more than a fiery death, had he ever figured out where Steve had disappeared to.

So, as much as I desired to fit in with the guys, my more feminine approach to play usually won out and was sometimes dictated by those boys that my mother often referred to as "neighborhoodlums." Wars were always breaking out on the bulge of grass behind the clothesline at the Kenneys' house that was the site of our Army battlefield. Cap guns, squirt guns, BB guns and slingshots were the weapons of war in epic days-long battles. As soon as breakfasts of Pop-Tarts and Tang were wolfed down, my brother would ring the dinner bell on our back porch as a call to arms and the boys would gather on the grassy knoll. Since my philosophy of war was "lie down and play dead until the danger passes," I was relegated to the M*A*S*H tent, a lean-to of plywood and branches propped up against the ivy-covered chain-link fence that marked the boundary between our yards.

In the relative safety of my tent, I awaited the arrival of soldiers seeking medical attention and dodged the occasional dirtball hand grenade. I was armed with Kleenex and masking tape to bandage up wounds and my gypsy scarves became slings and tourniquets. Injured troops could count on icy water served from my Girl Scout canteen and a stick of Beech-Nut Fruit Stripe gum as they went back to face the horrors of battle, taking cover in the thickets of honeysuckle and suffering the sharp stings in the blackberry-bush trenches.

Nursing was in my blood. My mother had gone to Kings County Hospital School of Nursing in Brooklyn and married my father the week after graduation. Though she lost her first job when they found out she was pregnant with me mere months after her honeymoon and never actually worked as a nurse again, her training was obvious in her skillful slathering of mercurochrome on our frequent cuts and scrapes or in coaxing a sick child through the god-awful rectal temperature taking—save for the time she got a phone call while I was flat on my stomach with my underwear pulled down to my knees, eventually falling into a fevered sleep then rolling over to nearly puncture my colon with my mercury and glass tail.

I found a better example of nursing on the rare occasions when I'd tune into M*A*S*H out of Mom's view. I thought Hot

Lips Houlihan had quite the life as an independent woman working alongside all those macho men. But if Mom caught us with that show on, she'd storm into the den and turn off the tv. "That inappropriately dressed Klinger character sets an appalling example for children!" she muttered on more than one occasion. I wouldn't be surprised if she wrote letters to CBS trying to get such smut off the air, or at least moved to a later time.

Yet I totally channeled my inner Hot Lips in my M*A*S*H tent, filling it with romance and intrigue. I had a crush on a boy who lived two blocks away, which meant I upped my own game when he joined in on our Army games, as the call to battle was generally only sounded off within the cluster of kid-filled houses along Old Farm Road. Michael and I were exactly the same age; as a matter of fact, we shared a birthday, which in my amorous idealism meant we were destined to be together.

When I heard the approach of an injured serviceman moaning in mock pain, I hoped the face coming through my pillowcase-covered door would be Michael's. When it was, I was particularly attentive, encouraging extra rest and multiple sips of water. I wiped his brow with a moistened tissue, trying not to get my pinky caught in one of the damp brown curls framing his angelic face. I was smitten, but my romantic reveries were always interrupted by the arrival of another thirsty soldier, often my brother, who I'm quite sure was on to my intentions and aimed to destroy my hopes of young love whenever possible.

And when the soldiers from both sides decided to attack my hospital tent with dirt clods and I was forced to flee as my fantasies crumbled into a pile of twigs and plywood, only to see Michael and my brother leading the charge, I learned quickly that there really is nothing fair in love or war.

CHAPTER TWELVE

Home Run

D addy sat in his recliner watching baseball as I pirouetted across the rug leaving a sprinkle of sequins in my wake and briefly blocking his view.

"Can't you do that somewhere else?" he grumbled, and I scampered away, seen but unseen.

My father was all about work, up before I rose in the morning and home just in time for dinner, after which he would retire to his recliner with a beer and turn the television on to sports or his favorite shows: *The Rockford Files* and *The Six Million Dollar Man*. When Dad was in his recliner, we knew he was not to be disturbed. Even if he was asleep and we'd sneak to the television set to turn the dial to *Little House on the Prairie*, Dad would jolt awake declaring, "I was just resting my eyes!" and we'd be forced to turn back to his show, even though his eyes would be closed and he'd be snoring again within five minutes.

But Tuesday? That was our night, because on Tuesdays, Daddy had his West Raleigh Exchange Club meetings and Mom would relax, sometimes even letting us eat TV dinners or SpaghettiOs from the can, and we could watch *Happy Days* and *Laverne & Shirley* without interruption.

Daddy's Exchange Club gave scholarships and created halls of American history at local schools, but their main project was running the Little League baseball program, in which almost all the boys in my neighborhood played. I'd been watching them throw balls with their dads in the street for years. I saw my father smiling at my brother as he tossed up pop flies and my brother grinning back when they landed square in his mitt. I wanted my dad to look at me that way.

I announced my intention at dinner one night when I was ten. Casual. Like asking someone to "Please pass the butter." I said, "So I think I'd like to play baseball this summer," and I scooped up a spoonful of peas.

"Girls don't play baseball," my brother scoffed with his mouthful of mashed potatoes.

"Well, of course they can," said my mother. "And don't talk with food in your mouth."

"Just because they can doesn't mean they should, and really they can't," said my brother.

"Girls play sports. Chris Evert is one of the best athletes in the world," said my mother.

"But I bet she can't hit a baseball," retorted my brother.

My father hadn't said a thing. I looked at him, hopeful, but he was focused on his plate.

"Girls can't run as fast as boys. It's a proven fact," my brother smirked, taking my father's silence as solidarity. "And those pitches are fast. Girls would cry if they got hit by a ball."

"You'd cry if you got hit, too," I countered, kicking him under the table. "I've seen you cry, you sissy!"

Mom glared, her lips pursed in that universal "mom look," meaning someone is about to get sent to their room without dessert. "Bill, don't you think Suzanne could join the team this year?"

"I guess I could ask," Dad responded, and my brother shot daggers my way with his eyes, and I melted them with my smile before they got anywhere near my force field.

And so, I became the first girl in the West Raleigh baseball program. But there was a problem. My brother was right. I couldn't play. In practice I rarely caught a ball and when I threw them back, they always landed yards in front of my target.

Our minor league team was the Mitchell's Hair Styling Dodgers and our sponsors paid for twelve sets of navy-blue polyester shirts with blue and white pin-striped pants. Problem was, we had fourteen players. When the coach passed out the uniforms, he handed me and another new kid, who was only eight, the plain white cotton and wool blend button-down jerseys and pants from the 1960s. I was devastated as I watched all the boys putting on their crisp new sponsor shirts. I was one of the oldest players on the team and I was new and I was a girl. I already stood out, and now I had to wear that stupid uniform. The humiliation was more than I could bear.

I sobbed all the way home, but a couple days later, my dad showed up before practice with pants that matched my brother's and a jersey that was similar to the rest of the team with my name screened onto the back. It was one of the nicest things anyone had ever done for me. He was my hero.

When the season began, I tucked my hair up into my hat and took my position in right field, but it was rare that anything was ever hit out there. I was bored. So I made clover necklaces and encircled my blue Dodgers cap with a crown of dandelions. True to my brother's prediction, I couldn't hit any better than I could throw. Every time I got up to bat, the coach would say, "Let it hit you!" so I could get on base before I struck out. And I did let it hit me. And it hurt. But I didn't cry.

Mostly, though, I spent my time sitting on the bench, trying to catch the eye of a cute boy from fifth grade and breathing in the scent of hotdogs from the snack bar where my dad sold Babe Ruth chocolate bars for fifteen cents and three Bazooka bubble gums for a nickel.

Every night I dreamt of hitting a home run over the Tastee Freez sign just below the scoreboard on the centerfield fence, partly to gain credibility for my sex, partly to see the look on my brother's face, and partly to make my father proud—but mostly for the free sundae the sign promised the person who hit a ball over the blue and white plywood placard.

"Home run! Suzanne Lowe!" In my dreams, I could hear the announcer call my name from the booth and the roar of the crowd in the bleachers. But that was not meant to be. I did, however, hit one ball that, with a series of *Bad News Bears* fielding errors, landed me on second base. Our side retired before I could score, but it felt so good to see the view from an infield bag with my hands buzzing from the bat connecting with a ball.

"That was a great hit," my dad said after the game, and I beamed at the recognition.

Sadly, though it had not been my goal, I was not a good example for the growing women's lib movement as my participation drew ire from at least one concerned citizen who wrote to the *Raleigh Times* demanding that girls not be allowed on boys' teams. But the 1974 National Organization for Women lawsuit had forced National Little League to revise their rules and allow girls into the sport. Maybe I cracked the dugout ceiling so that the girls who came after me, the ones who were playing with a true passion for baseball, could earn that Tastee Freez sundae and much more.

While my non-heroic baseball career ended that season and my crowning achievement was a ring of clover around my cap, my father clearly appreciated my chutzpah and for me, that was a home run.

CHAPTER THIRTEEN
The Clue in the Breakwater

I blame it on Nancy Drew. I was impressionable. I was looking for a strong female role model. And I craved adventure. She was a girl sleuth who embodied moxie and independence. She went on interesting escapades and solved complicated puzzles.

I was ten when I picked up my first mystery book, *The Secret of the Old Clock*, and I was hooked. For every holiday over several years, all I wanted was more Nancy Drew books. I saved my money and meticulously added to my collection. The yellow spines lined my bookshelf next to my Madame Alexander *Little Women* and Scarlett O'Hara dolls.

As I read *The Sign of the Twisted Candles* and learned *The Password to Larkspur Lane*, I began to see myself as our neighborhood's detective, recognizing pretty much everything around me as potentially suspicious. A misplaced box of cereal in the cookie aisle at the grocery store was surely a clue to an intriguing caper. The milkman clearly looked shady, and I was certain that he was smuggling something contraband next to the milk in that orange Pine State truck.

Letters might be hidden in library books that could lead to unclaimed treasures. I began burying clues in my own diaries in case something ever happened to me so that the Raleigh police department would have solid leads in their investigation. *Look closely at Tommy Kenney,* I wrote. *I saw him carrying a heavy box into his house yesterday. His eyes were shifty. I think he is up to something.*

Nancy Drew's mysteries absorbed most of my spare time from age ten to thirteen, at which point I became more interested in real boys than in hoping that Nancy would finally kiss dreamy Ned Nickerson.

When I was twelve, my family took our annual summer trip to Emerald Isle. Daddy's work buddy once again lent us the lower-level apartment of his celadon-green, cement-block beach house. From there, it was a short walk through the Peppertree condo complex up to the big gazebo that stood proudly between two dunes, with showers on the stair landings so you could get the sand off yourself and your beach toys before heading back to the surely plush, shag-carpeted, air-conditioned heaven that I imagined a Peppertree condo promised.

Our accommodations were not all that impressive, but Mom would remind us that we were lucky to even *be* at the beach and if we felt like complaining about the musky mildew smell that greeted us when we kicked open the warped front door, we *could* be camping back at Salter Path in a cramped tent.

And we'd shut up, because we *were* grateful for the cool linoleum floors and the bathroom where you didn't have to pay a quarter for a shower or risk peeing on a patch of poison oak under a Loblolly pine behind the picnic table.

A plaque along the beach path near our basement apartment indicated that Blackbeard's ship, the *Queen Anne's Revenge,* was believed to have run aground on a sandbar off the coast not far from where we were. As I lay on my towel reading *The Mystery of the Tolling Bell,* my mind drifted to swashbuckling pirates and the possibility of hidden treasure along the Bogue Banks. I asked my mother if I could take a walk and I headed out toward the jetty.

I was about two hundred yards from my father, who was sitting in his yellow mesh folding chair, ankle deep in the water attempting to lure the speckled trout that might be our dinner, when I saw it: a greened-bronze rectangle at the end of the L-shaped fork in the jetty. As the tide ebbed, it was clear there were words on it. I was certain that those words were a clue that would lead to a treasure, possibly something valuable from the *Queen Anne's Revenge.*

I climbed up on the first of the dozen or so large concrete blocks that made up the breakwater. Barnacles crunched below my feet as I walked to the next eight-foot-long block. I looked back to see my mother in a distant beach chair, and my brother and little sister hunched over a sandcastle.

The next jetty blocks were cool and damp from the splash of the tides, and the block after those felt good on my feet with mossy green algae covering the barnacles. I was getting closer to the end, where the wall turned to make the L-shaped blockade, but I still couldn't make out any of the words. Suddenly, I slipped, slamming my knee into the cement as I slid off the left side of the barrier wall. My family was on the right.

I struggled for footing and a place to grip the wall as a big wave came in, smashing my head against the jetty. I tried to swim out from the breakwater, but each wave pushed me back against the wall.

My feet found a rather large rock, and I was finally able to rest my legs and assess the situation. The wall was covered in mussels, making it difficult to cling to. There was no way I could climb up it. Jumping on the rock, I could barely wave my hand above it. There were no people visible on the beach save for a fisherman in the distance where the barrier island curved toward the inlet. But when I shouted as loud as I could for help, he didn't move, the sound of the waves surely drowning my voice.

The tide was rising and my rock perch was quickly becoming deeper. Water that was at first just below my shoulders as the tides receded was now almost to my chin. As a big wave came crashing in, I had time for a deep breath, but I hadn't braced myself. I slipped off the rock and my ankle slid between it and the wall, lodging my foot in the gap. I was below water level, running out of air fast in my panic.

Just then a hand gripped my arm, pulling me up. But my foot was still stuck. I twisted and squirmed and somehow wrangled free as my guardian angel grabbed for my other hand and pulled my scraped-up body to the surface of the jetty.

The angel fisherman had seen me walking along the breakwater and glanced back to see that I was no longer there. He briefly thought his eyes were playing tricks on him in the bright July sunlight, but instinct told him, "Go check just in case." He faintly heard my call and saw my hand pop above the wall as he navigated the slippery rocks.

He cautiously carried me across the wall toward my family. Mom raced over to take me from his arms, thanking him profusely. I was crying as my father approached the towels.

"What in the heck were you doing that far out on the rocks?" he yelled.

"I was trying to solve a mystery," I whimpered. "There is a clue on the plaque at the end of the jetty and I just wanted to see what it says."

"I'll tell you right now what it says," grumbled my dad. "Slippery when wet."

CHAPTER FOURTEEN
Spin the Bottle

The Cheerwine bottle spun on the checkers board in the middle of the shag carpet in Michael's basement as a dozen shiny-faced twelve and thirteen-year-olds sat Indian-style in a circle around it, looking on with a palpable blend of hope and dread.

It was my first boy-girl party and I know the only reason Mom let me go was because it was at the Kelly's house and Mrs. Kelly was a regular at St. Michael's Catholic Church. Mom figured nothing untoward would happen in a good Catholic home. Mom, however, had not set foot in the den of iniquity that was the Kelly's dimly lit basement. She'd only been in Mrs. Kelly's cozy living room with crocheted doilies on the tables and the handknit afghan draped over Mr. Kelly's Barcalounger to hide the oil stain from his Brylcreem. Mom and the other church ladies would gather in each other's living rooms every Wednesday morning to discuss the catechism over cups of tea and delicate Moravian cookies and, in hushed voices, the sinful goings-on in the homes of our Baptist neighbors. "Bless her heart," they'd say, preceding each unkind comment.

On the afternoon of the party, Mrs. Richman, a Methodist, came by to cut my hair in our kitchen. None of the Catholics we knew could come close to her talent with scissors and a comb. I'd grown out my flat attempt at the Dorothy Hamill wedge and wanted more of a modern Kristy McNichol shag. Mom spread the *Raleigh Times* over the linoleum floor and Mrs. Richman got out her professional shears. As clumps of my mousy hair fell atop Margaret Thatcher's face, I prayed that my new haircut would make me pretty and I'd be propelled from dull anonymity to someone boys might actually notice.

But when I looked in the downstairs bathroom mirror, I was not pretty. I looked like Rod Stewart had cut his own hair and couldn't reach the back. I was early to the coming mullet fad.

I had no time to request a new look. The party was starting in half an hour. I raced upstairs and put on my bell-bottom jeans. Now, my legs were growing far faster than the rest of me, so Mom tried to extend the life of my jeans by letting out the hem, which at first looked kind of cool with the gradations of blue and the fraying edges along the bottom. That is, until a few weeks later, when my mother decided to make them "cooler" while showing off her newly acquired needlepoint skills. She embroidered a swirling vine of lumpy roses and sunflowers around the bottom of the legs, ostensibly to mask the obvious lines where the hem had been let out. In the '60s this might have been groovy. But this was 1979! These pants were just plain dorky. Then, to add insult to injury, Mom decided to add words. She stitched along the bottom of each leg, *Man O Man Suzanne.*

She was so proud of her handiwork and didn't want to leave my brother out of her couture design. To the back of his favorite jeans jacket she replicated the swirling flower pattern and added *Billy the Kidd* in bright red stitching. He never wore that jacket again.

I pulled on a red sweater with blue and white stripes, but realized you can't go to a boy-girl party without a bra and I didn't have one yet. Always a resourceful problem solver, I put on my navy-blue bikini top dotted with white ship wheels and anchors that was more of a cropped tank, but at least there were bra-like lines under my sweater. Surely the basement would be too dark for anyone to notice the nautical symbols through the red knit.

My palms were sweating as I knocked on the Kelly's door, hoping Mrs. Kelly would recognize my maturity immediately. I was no longer the tomgirl who played football and Army with her sons. I'd graduated way beyond making clover necklaces in the outfield in West Raleigh Little League. This right here was the big leagues. This was where you decided if you were going to be a Sandy or a Rizzo.

Of course, if my mother had her way, that thought would never have entered my mind. She forbade me from seeing *Grease* when it came out the previous summer. It was an inappropriate story about a good girl gone bad and she didn't want me to get any ideas. But our neighbor, Mrs. Lucas, invited me over for a slumber party and then took us to the Mission Valley Theatre.

"But my mom will be mad," I weakly protested as Lynn and I jumped into the back seat with our Ziploc baggies filled with Jiffy Pop.

"Oh, your mother is being silly. This is one of those times where you don't ask for permission and just ask for forgiveness later."

If that was a Baptist mantra, I liked it. Catholics live with too much fear.

At the top of the steps leading to Michael's basement, there was a cross and the same "Head of Christ" painting that greeted me each morning when I opened my bedroom door to see Jesus bathed in soft light and looking toward the heavens. Rumor was we'd be playing *Seven Minutes in Heaven,* and I had a decision to make. Was I Sandra Dee or a Pink Lady? I descended the steps.

The basement was nothing like the rest of the house. The dark wood-paneled walls were covered in The Doors and Pink

Floyd posters and adorned with multi-colored Christmas lights.

Kids were sitting on the shag carpet or draped over the arms of the couch. Michael was by the turntable trying to decide between *Double Vision* and *Frampton Comes Alive*. I casually made my way to the snack table and grabbed a handful of Cheese Puffs while I sized up the room. There were a couple girls I remembered from first communion classes and a few other neighborhood kids, but no one mattered to me as much as Michael. I was plotting my path to the turntable when Michelle took charge. She directed us to sit boy-girl-boy-girl in a circle and put the checkers board in the middle, bulls-eyed by the bottle. As she explained the rules, my stomach did backflips. This could be my chance at a first kiss. This could be my chance to prove my love to Michael.

Michelle spun first. The bottle landed on Beth. Of course Michelle spun again; girls didn't kiss girls. This time it landed on a boy in an NC State sweatshirt. The two went to the closet with the louvered doors. Everyone oohed as the door slid closed and the light went out. A few minutes later, they came out without looking at each other. When the boy sat next to me, his face was as red as his sweatshirt.

Another boy spun the bottle and I crossed my fingers, praying it wouldn't land on me. The rules strictly prohibited going into the closet a second time until everyone had a turn. It stopped on a girl in a purple velour tracksuit. Everyone giggled as they ducked into the closet. They stayed even longer. I think her jacket might have been zipped a little lower when she came out. She was clearly a Rizzo.

Then it was my turn. I took a deep breath and prayed like I never prayed before. I prayed more deeply than I'd prayed that my sister would be born a sister. I prayed more deeply than I'd prayed that we wouldn't be bombed by Russia. I prayed more deeply than I had that Giselle wouldn't get her period before I did.

Holy Moly! Praying worked! The bottle turned twice and God came through as it pointed directly at the boy of my dreams. Like a gentleman, Michael opened the accordion closet door and let me walk in first. I could feel his eyes on me in the dark. I could hear my heart beating against my bikini top but I didn't know what to do. I wanted to wrap my arms around him and plant a big kiss on his lips. But I stood there as a cold sweat crept through my sweater. I didn't move. Michael didn't move. Someone said, "I wonder what's going on in there?" and everyone laughed. Michael finally broke the impasse and kissed me lightly on the cheek, then opened the door and we nonchalantly assumed our seats in the circle as the game moved on. I kept trying to catch his eyes in the glow of the Christmas lights, hoping that his heart had skipped a beat like my own and that he, too, hoped for another chance. But I saw nothing.

In the end, I guess I went into the closet and Sandra Dee emerged, still hopelessly devoted and longing for love's first kiss.

CHAPTER FIFTEEN
Cotton Baller

The way that adults think of traffic school is the way I thought of junior high school physical education. A necessary evil. Something you had to complete to move forward with your life. Hell.

Our uniforms were goldenrod t-shirts and our names were written in Sharpie under the kelly-green mascot insignia. We were the Imps—a little devil essentially—and in the southern accents of our cheerleaders, that four-letter word was two syllables: Ee-Yimps. Our shorts were stiff green with yellow piping and a rigid two-inch elastic waistband.

At thirteen and fourteen, most of the girls were wearing bras and many needed them, too. I was not one of the lucky ones. One of the boys in science class nicknamed me "Minnesota Flats." "Chairman of the Board of the Itty-Bitty Titty Committee," declared another. I begged my mother for a bra, complaining about how embarrassing it was changing in front of the other girls and being the only one with nothing on but a lacy tank top adorned with a flower and a bow in front. But the truth was that I *never* undressed in front of anyone.

I tiptoed into the bathroom stall to change and promptly flushed the unused toilet as I left with my clothes balled up as tightly as possible so no one would know I was too shy to change at my locker in front of Heather, with her perky breasts hidden under a lacy bra, or Aisha, with her huge chocolate boobs spilling out of a Playtex Torpedo definitely bigger than my mother's.

Mom finally gave in and took me to Belk to pick out a Teenform "training bra" in size 32AA. "You're trying to grow up too fast," my mother grumbled as she paid two dollars for the yellow box with my new bra inside. But it wasn't the game changer I'd hoped it would be. I was still flat as a board, so I tried filling my bra with socks, toilet paper and cotton balls to see what I might look like when my real breasts came in. Cotton seemed to give the most realistic look, but that meant that I still had to change in the bathroom lest someone discover that I was a "stuffer."

One day, when clouds ominously threatened rain, our teacher, Miss Hill, kept the class inside the gym. The boys were instructed to take over one basketball court while the girls were sent to the other. Miss Hill was a tall, thin black woman who dyed her hair red and never shaved her legs. I had yet to shave my legs either, but the thick, curly hair on Miss Hill's legs was the subject of countless jokes on the rare occasions when she chose to wear shorts instead of sweatpants.

As I sat on the court waiting for Miss Hill to launch the boys' game with a jump ball, I self-consciously realized that I actually did have noticeably fuzzy hair on my kneecaps. I discreetly glanced around the room and observed that most of the other girls' legs appeared shaven, at least from the knees down. They also all had pierced ears. I had to wait until I was sixteen to get my ears pierced. I decided that night to stealthily borrow my dad's razor and definitely not mention it to my mother.

Miss Hill's whistle brought me out of my self-image trance. The woman was lazy. Instead of picking the teams herself, she chose two team captains and let them do the dirty work. One captain was one of the most popular girls in school. A cheerleader, Betsy Jones was perky, with a dimpled smile, and clothes right off the pages of *Seventeen* magazine. The other captain was a known nerd. Karen Neely wore smudged glasses and dark knee socks with her gym uniform. She was in my English and math classes and always seemed to have all the answers. In an effort to not be typecast as a nerd, I never attempted to befriend Karen Neely, but with my luck, I was quite sure I'd end up on her team.

The captains chose their friends first and then picked their friends' friends. Each time Betsy's turn came, she'd take whispered recommendations from her *Heathers*-meets-*Mean Girls* entourage. Then she'd come out of the huddle and announce with great pride, "We choose Mary Catherine!" And a beautiful blonde sauntered to center court. As the remaining girls waiting to be chosen dwindled, I began to get nervous. *Had they noticed me? Was I invisible?* I'd been in class with both these girls at Kingswood for sixth grade. "Hey! It's me! Please choose me. Please choose me. *Please choose me!*" I frantically screamed over and over in my head. Then I got really nervous.

There were only five girls left. It was Karen's turn. "I pick Holly." My heart dropped to my stomach as a girl with an afro and thick Coke-bottle glasses walked to the left side of the court.

"The girl in the Converse," Betsy announced after a brief consultation with her beautiful teammates. Great, now they were beyond names. They'd moved on to distinguishing features and we were all wearing gym clothes. I probably hadn't brushed my mousy hair that morning. Uggh! I knew I was in trouble as I looked down at my plain white "Keds-a-likes" from Kmart paired with red and white striped NC State gym socks. They were my lucky socks in fifth grade when the Wolfpack won the National Championship, but they'd lost their elastic along with their luck and were bunched up around my ankles on this fateful day in seventh.

Only three girls were left.

I looked kindly at Karen to try and create a sense of familiarity. *Remember that time we ate at the same table in sixth grade? Remember when I picked up your pencil in math?* I tried to speak what was in my heart with my friendly, hopeful eyes.

But Karen Neely chose Karen Yankolowitz. Name similarity. Who could blame her? Now it was down to me and a pale girl with bowl-cut red hair whom I'd actually never even noticed in class before. Betsy pointed and said "You."

Her index finger was like the hand of a clock between numbers, yet it seemed directed at me and I took a relieved step forward. The other girl, however, was already sprinting to the "Eee-Yimp" in center court. The teams were clustered together and Mrs. Hill signaled for me to go to a group, but I couldn't tell which one.

Yet out of the darkness came a little burst of hope. If I play well, they'll fight over who has me and I am pretty good at P-I-G with my brother in the cul-de-sac. Just then, a miracle happened. The ball bounced into my hands. I dribbled it once. I dribbled it twice, and I shot it toward the hoop. And like a slow-motion moment in *Hoosiers,* the ball soared through the air and swooshed right into the basket.

I anticipated cheers. A pat on the back? But there was only silence. Until an argument broke out between the ten players on the court. It seems I wasn't actually in the game and therefore the basket didn't count. I was sure, though, that they'd now be anxious to have me on their teams. A great shot like myself? Yet they went on playing and I was still unsure of which sideline I should go to. I grabbed a bathroom pass off the wall by the stack of green and white gymnastics mats and hid in the stall for the rest of the period. And when the bell rang, I wiped the tears from my cheeks, adjusted my cotton balls, and held my head up high. I'd even the score with those girls some other time. Right then and there, I basked in my private glory. Nothing but net! Nothing but net.

CHAPTER SIXTEEN
Dust in the Wind

The adults sat in a stiff semicircle in the living room, balancing cups and saucers on their knees and nibbling on mini banana nut muffins from the rose-patterned china platter on the coffee table, the scents of Aqua Net and Jean Naté mingled with the apple-cinnamon air freshener my mother had hastily spritzed around the entryway before the guests began to arrive.

One by one, I could see them from my perch in my bedroom window, somberly parading up the driveway with casserole dishes in hand draped in dishtowels or wrapped in foil to keep them warm. A basket covered in a red and white checked cloth napkin rocked on the wrist of the gray-haired lady who sang too loudly at church, a potted violet in her opposite hand tilted precariously as bits of soil bounced off her stiff black shoe.

I could hear them talking in hushed tones that rose and fell with occasional bursts of laughter followed by awkward silence. A shiny black car appeared in the cul-de-sac and pulled up behind a dusty green Impala parked in front of our house. A man climbed out wearing a black suit, leaned down into the front seat, donned his fedora, and picked up a white box about the size of a lunch box. It could have held a telephone for my room or maybe the brown leather purse we saw at Hudson Belk the weekend before last.

I rushed downstairs and opened the door just as the man rapped his knuckle once against the screen.

"Is your mother home?" he asked.

"She is currently occupied with company," I stated as maturely as possible, eyeing the box.

"I have something I need for her to sign for," he said.

"I can do it," I declared, still hopeful. "Today is my thirteenth birthday, so I'm old enough."

Perhaps my confidence impressed him, or maybe he was just in a hurry, because moments later I was neatly writing my name on a tiny line just as I'd practiced in the margins of my math book thousands of times before, in case I ever became famous. He handed me the box, tipped his hat, and said, "My condolences."

Like the messages on most of the cards that covered the piano casting their shadows over my birthday cards: *With Deepest Sympathy. Our thoughts and prayers are with you. Our hearts go out to you in this time of loss.*

The box was warm. Clearly not the phone or the purse. Maybe fresh chocolate chip cookies? Was I so wrong to think that maybe someone would remember that today was my birthday?

Mom was all puffy-eyed sitting at the kitchen table when I came downstairs in the morning. She made no effort to make me my favorite breakfast and didn't even ask if I felt any older today like she had every birthday morning I could remember over the past dozen years. There weren't any packages or cards or balloons at my seat at the kitchen table and instead of asking what kind of cake I wanted, she barked out orders about vacuuming and cleaning the toilets.

So yeah, while my mother stood in the kitchen surrounded by her friends and a counter full of casseroles, I walked up to her with the warm white box and said, "A man just dropped this off.

Can I open it?" And my mother, scattered and spent, distracted and unthinking said, "Sure." And I grabbed a knife from the butcher's block and cut the gold seal and opened the box of...

A gasp came over my left shoulder, and the cacophony of voices and silverware clicking against plates suddenly stopped. All eyes were on me. Someone on my right took the warm box out of my hand. Turns out it wasn't a gift for me at all.

It was such a small box, really. A small box filled with probably less ash and soot than sat below the grate of our fireplace. Five or six cups' worth and my grandmother, Madeline Gladys Flynn McGrath, was five-foot-six. "Gladys with the Gorgeous Gams" they called her in her flapper days. I've seen the photos of her in fabulous fringe dresses with a cloche hat and perfect pin curls like a character from *The Great Gatsby*, leaning against the running board of a cool black Cadillac and smiling conspiratorially. What was she up to? I never thought to ask.

She was an old lady when I knew her, but I didn't really know her. My mother's stories of her own mother were more about the time they spent in church. She shared so little about what it was like growing up in Brooklyn. Her much older siblings had left home when my mother was still quite young. And now my mother was motherless in this month of Mother's Day and all I could think of was, "Shouldn't being the mother of *me* be enough? Shouldn't having had *me* thirteen years ago today count for something?"

Yet there I stood in the kitchen as a neighbor put the box on the counter and hugged my mother. And I stared in disbelief. How could the granddaughter of Irish farmers who crossed through Ellis Island during the potato famine—the youngest of thirteen children who grew up in the midst of the Great Depression, raised three children including one with polio, a woman who wore clip-on earrings, gray-blonde wigs and Norell perfume, and once played the bongo drums alongside her husband in the Capitol Towers retirement home band—be reduced to half of a cubic foot?

Number seven on Casey Kasem's Top Forty that week was Kansas' "Dust in the Wind" and I didn't really believe that was all we were until I held that box of Grandma on my thirteenth birthday.

CHAPTER SEVENTEEN
Pain and Novocaine

Our scars are songs written on our skin, singing their mournful or joyous melodies through their lingering marks. Among the many dings on my epidermis, my left knee is the first refrain I can remember, holding lyrics bone deep from that time when I Evil Knievel-ed my brand-new ten-speed bike down the hill of our cul-de-sac. I got going too fast to check for oncoming traffic, overcorrected, and hit the asphalt, hard. There I lay in the middle of Old Farm Road on my twelfth birthday, grateful to see my father heading toward me, a giant shadow silhouetted against the cloudless May sky.

Yelling. My father was yelling. Maybe to alert oncoming traffic? But no, there wasn't a car in sight. He was yelling at me.

"I go and get you a nice new bike and this is what you do with it?" he screamed as he picked up my shiny blue bicycle with the now crooked seat and scuffed handlebars. Dad stormed off carrying the bike and left me crying and bloody in the street.

When I limped into the kitchen, my mother tenderly wiped the blood from my shin and picked the gravel bits from my kneecap.

"Your father just doesn't know how to express love," she said as she coated the deep wound with mercurochrome and Neosporin and wrapped my leg with gauze.

Well, he sure knows how to show love for a bike, I thought.

I spent the rest of the afternoon watching an Afterschool Special, "The Tap Dance Kid," on the couch as the smell of a Betty Crocker cake baked in the oven. In the movie, big sister Emma stands up against her parents' stringent rules and launches a "Children's Rights Crusade." That girl was on to something and she totally spoke to my sense of justice. But the star of the show was her little brother, Willie, whose Broadway-caliber tap-dancing skills most captured my imagination.

That summer, I decided that I, too, wanted to learn to tap dance. I'd taken ballet when I was younger but hadn't danced for several years. Mom agreed to sign me up for a class at Suzie Kovack's Academy. But the first step to tap steps was tap shoes. We pulled up to Relevé Dancewear in Cameron Village, my toes percolating with excitement. I was so eager to find my rhythm, to let my heart beat in my feet and to stomp out my frustrations.

But when they measured me, it turned out the only shoes they had in stock were a half-size too small. I Cinderella's stepsister-ed those shoes and claimed they fit just fine because I knew my mother. If the mission took too much effort, she'd abort. The only other dance shoe store was way across town. Granted, I later learned that if you took the freeway, it only took about fifteen minutes to get there, but by using surface streets as Mom always did, the forty-five-minute drive was daunting. It was either these shoes or no tap.

And so, I was terrible at tap. Every shuffle-ball-change was an exercise in pain. By the time the recital came in the spring, my shoes were surely a whole size too small. I faked a toothy smile as I flapped and brushed, cramped and step-heeled in my neon pink and yellow attention-grabbing costume with equally neon pink blisters bulging on my heels, a joyful experiment turned torturous.

The following spring, my pain took a new turn. Previous wounds did not compare. As our dentist, Dr. Brooks, picked and prodded at my molars, I should have known. I'd made it to thirteen without a cavity. That day he found two. I blame it on the big bag of saltwater taffy we got on a beach trip that summer.

"I hate to be the bearer of bad news," he said to my mother in the waiting room. They discussed whether he should do the dental work now or schedule a follow-up visit.

"Let's get it over with," Mom said as she got out her checkbook, a side-eyed glare directed toward me, still in the dental chair across the hall. She, however, refused to sign off on the use of Novocaine. She said it was because she'd had an adverse reaction many years back and didn't trust the medication. And she said she didn't want her child drugged. Dr. Brooks said he wouldn't advise such an approach, but agreed to rub my gums with numbing gel.

I think Mom thought fear of pain was a good deterrent to the cost of future fillings. Whatever the truth was, the sound of the drill is as high-pitched as the pain that is etched into my jaws and my consciousness: searing, intense, radiating and mind-numbing. I grew up knowing that were I ever to get another cavity, I would have to undergo the repair without a painkiller. Mom was right, fear did make me diligent about brushing my teeth.

And yes, the fear of pain is a great deterrent, but actual pain is even better. It can keep you from conquering hills at breakneck speed, dancing with abandon, and from eating saltwater taffy. But many scars are more than skin deep and leave you longing to be picked up when you fall and craving relief from the pain.

CHAPTER EIGHTEEN
Life, Edited

We're in the basement of my uncle's house in Mason, Ohio. It is the summer of 1979 and I am thirteen years old. My Uncle Tom is a vibrant, vociferous storyteller who resembles Santa Claus. The proud father of six, he is generous with gifts and hugs, and the house is buzzing with excitement as plans are coming together for his eldest daughter, my cousin Maureen's, wedding.

This is only the second time I can recall ever seeing my cousins and I am overjoyed at the feeling of connection with these distant people who are my family. The first time I met them, I was five and we were in Brooklyn visiting my grandparents. I remember going to the Bronx Zoo, Grandpa holding my hand on one side and my cousin Michael's, the youngest of Uncle Tom's brood, on the other. My mother is pushing my baby brother in the red umbrella stroller with my grandmother by their side. Grandpa had purchased a bag of lollipops and given it to me to dole out. I imagine my older cousins were not pleased at the pint-sized keeper of the treats. I imagine I was economical with my generosity; after all, unlike my cousins, I came from a frugal home.

Later Uncle Tom took us all out to a big dinner in Little Italy with the longest table I'd ever seen filled with fourteen people that I was related to, and there was so much food and loud conversation. It was what I imagined family dinners were like when

Scrooge looked in at Fezziwig's. I asked my parents often if we could go see my cousins again, and Mom repeatedly said, "One day," but it only happened when there was a wedding and then we were always part of a blur of other activities.

Ten years older than my mother, Uncle Tom started his family before my mother was a teen. Because of the age difference, they'd never been very close, so as adults, it was more than the ten hours of driving distance that kept them apart.

"Tom drinks too much," I heard my mother tell my father as they planned our trip to Maureen's wedding eight years after that trip to New York. "Maybe we can get a motel so we can have a little peace and quiet?" she suggested.

"They invited us to stay with them," my father countered, "and it will save us a lot of money if we do."

And so, it was settled. We loaded up the LTD and with my baby sister sitting in her carrier between my parents and my brother and I sprawled out in the back with piles of pillows and coloring books, mouths full of Pop Rocks and Nancy Drew and the Hardy Boys to keep us company, we set out through the rolling hills where Mt. Airy leads into Virginia through the New River Gorge, across West Virginia, and on to Ohio.

We arrived late in the afternoon, and Uncle Tom was already setting up for a feast in his yard. The scent of charcoal greeted us as soon as we piled out of the car and my cousins rushed up to see us. Their house was huge, with a full basement, off of which were the two rooms where we'd be sleeping.

After the boisterous BBQ, people congregated in the basement to play pool and continue the festivities at the well-stocked bar. My cousins began sharing stories of my grandparents: how Grandma made them change clothes at the beach with no privacy even after the girls were well into their teens, how Grandpa once got drunk and dangled my mother out the third-story window of their Brooklyn brownstone to stop my grandmother from harassing him about his drinking, how Grandma always burnt her pot roasts and tried to pass frozen Pepperidge Farm cakes off as homemade after she thawed them on one of her Wedgwood plates in the pantry. They lovingly shared story after hilarious story of how imperfect my grandma was while we giggled at their reflections.

Grandma McGrath had died just a few months earlier, and my mother had always portrayed her as a practically perfect saint. I began to think maybe there was more to the story of who my grandmother really was.

Later that evening, Mom came into the office where my brother and I were sleeping on a sofa bed to tuck us in.

"Don't believe a single word your uncle Tom said about your grandmother, kids. None of that nonsense is true. Your uncle is known for making up stories, and clearly, he has passed that nasty trait on to his children," she said matter-of-factly.

Mom reminded us of all the pious actions of her mother through the years. She detailed her devotion to the Father, Son and Holy Spirit. She asked us to kneel by our sofa bed to say our evening prayers and guided those prayers to include my uncle and cousins, who clearly needed forgiveness for their defective imaginations.

Decades later, as my mother was on her own deathbed, she began to plant memories of her own piety that reminded me of the seeds she was sowing with Grandma's legacy that night in the basement. As we reflected on my childhood, she steered the conversation toward my first communion and confirmation, toward time spent in Sunday school and catechism class. Mom knew I was no longer connected to the church and had fervently hoped she'd be cured of the cancer that now riddled her body in such a way that her heathen children would be so moved by the miracle that we'd all return to the church. Sadly for her, if her goal in life was to raise more Catholics, she had not succeeded.

CHAPTER NINETEEN
Guns and Gravel

I was out cold on the gravel driveway, with small chunks of rock embedded in my skull. A gun was lying next to me. The hot sun beat down on my face and I tried to open my eyes, the bright afternoon blocked by shadowy faces looking down at me.

"Are you ok?" they asked.

I vaguely remember hearing someone scream for ice and a towel. Maybe someone yelled "Call 911!" That could have just been my imagination. I don't remember an ambulance ever coming.

The rifle lying next to me was the second gun I'd ever held. The first gun was one I discovered in our house back when I was eleven. My parents would often leave me at home to watch my nine and one-year-old siblings, but rarely was I ever home alone. Perhaps they felt it was safer if we all were together, though I'd been known to drop the baby. A haphazard trip over the corner of a rug, or I'd reach out to answer the phone on the hallway wall, forgetting she was in my arms. Poor thing was often crying in my presence. Grandma said it was jealousy. Dad called me klutzy, but I'd grown up a lot in a year and hadn't dropped my sister in several months. Plus, my babysitting was cheap, as in they never paid me a cent.

On the day I found the gun, I was miraculously alone in our usually bustling house. My brother was on a Boy Scout trip, Dad was at work, and Mom had taken the baby to the doctor for a checkup (not because of anything I'd done to her). Naturally, when I knew the coast was clear, I went into my parents' upstairs bedroom seeking out the air conditioner with the cool hum that often lulled me into a rare, blissful summer nap if I was lucky enough to sneak time to myself in their room. It was about as close to heaven as one could get in that sticky, hot house on the cul-de-sac in West Raleigh.

As I lay there with my skinny, tanned legs stretched across the star-patterned bedspread that Grandma had quilted with her own arthritic hands, my eyes landed on Mom's jewelry box atop the dresser. I pretty much knew what was in there, having sat next to her as she took out her pearls to wear for Mass on many a Sunday. I'd tried on her ring from St. Francis Xavier High, class of 1962, twisted rosary beads into bracelets, and put on the mood ring she'd gotten in the late Sixties when I was a baby. She said her mood was always a bright, happy pink when I was around but whenever she put it on in my presence, I watched it turn a deep purplish black, signifying stress.

The dresser had six drawers, and I was curious what secrets might lie within. I quickly discovered that four of them were Mom's. I knew the bottom-left drawer was where she kept her slips and nightgowns because just about every Halloween when she helped me create my gypsy costumes, I used layers of those slips coupled with her scarves, Grandma's most gaudy clip-on earrings, and the Mardi Gras beads one of Daddy's coworkers brought back from a trip to New Orleans. I'd find out three years later why she bothered to keep a drawer full of maternity clothes when another baby came along.

I quickly closed Dad's underwear drawer with an audible "Eew!" But it was Dad's bottom-right drawer that intrigued me. Under several neatly folded sweaters was a thin cardboard box full of patches and pins from his days in the Navy, along with a scattering of gray-blue squares that I later learned were Trojan condoms that had expired in 1969. Beneath the patches and some military documents was a binder filled with Vargas pin-up girl paintings, torn from *Playboy* magazines. My eyes grew big as saucers as I took in the pictures of the naked centerfolds and the realization that my father had such a collection yet chose to marry a woman who was a fan of full-coverage bras and opaque high-rise cotton panties.

And on that day, when the outside air was thick with the scent of honeysuckle and the sweat of neighborhood kids playing war with squirt guns and water balloons in the yards encircling the cul-de-sac, I was to learn even more shocking details about my father's secret life as I rifled through his belongings in climate-controlled bliss. I heard a bang like a door closing in the distance and neatly but hastily placed the box under Dad's red Mr. Rogers-style cardigan and ran across the hall to see if my family was home. No sign of the Ford LTD.

I returned to my Nancy Drew sleuthing and felt under the thick Shetland wool pullover Daddy bought when he was stationed in Scotland. Spicy mothballs rolled across the bottom of the drawer as I came upon a small, hard case and when I snapped it open, I discovered a gun. My father had a gun! Was it possible that he was a secret agent and his supposed job at BellSouth was just a cover?

I could never confront my parents because I'd have to admit to snooping. Scenarios of Dad's secret life played out in my head as I eventually dozed off with a stripe of the afternoon sun melting across the quilt and my cut-off jean shorts. I awoke to the definitive slam of our front door and scrambled to get the gun securely into its gun-shaped foam space as a bag full of small yellow bullets spilled out all over the bed and rolled onto the floor.

I picked up as many as I could and kicked the rest under the bed, vowing to collect them later. I knew an offer to vacuum would always be joyfully greeted by my mom, but I'd have to keep the baby off the floor long enough to casually make that proposal.

I didn't realize until many years later, after fantasies of my father's secret spy career had long since fizzled, that the gun was a pellet gun and he could no more have joined James Bond in a car chase down Hillsborough Street than he could have protected our house with it.

Then came my friend's thirteenth birthday party at the farmhouse two summers later. There'd been barbeque, potato salad and salty green beans. A dozen teens sat in a circle under the sycamore tree throwing the spiky balls at each other and drinking cans of Cheerwine and Tab. Michelle was picking long strips of dead sunburned skin off Russell's back as Peter scratched at the mosquito bites on his legs until they bled. Julie's dad must have seen that we were bored and suggested we might like to do some shooting at the range. The boys jumped up immediately, kicking up dust as they followed Mr. Henderson down the gravel driveway, a rifle slung over his shoulder like he was heading off for war.

The "range" turned out to be a wood fence with a pyramid of Budweiser cans stacked on the top rail. Mr. Henderson told all the kids to step back as he took aim and fired. *Bam!* The sound echoed across the field, bouncing off the surrounding trees as the top can went flying and the whole tower crumbled. "Well, I'll be!" shouted Mr. Henderson with pride as Julie's little brother ran across the field to rebuild the pyramid and came back with the victim can, a hole clean through the round Anheuser-Busch insignia.

After all the boys had their turns, the kickback nearly jolting the skinniest guys off their feet, none of the girls stepped up. Julie was sitting on one of the boulder-like rocks that lined the drive rolling her eyes, the afternoon sun baking us all as we squinted, sweat dripping down our foreheads and precariously perching atop our brows.

I didn't like seeing girls being sissies, so I stood up from my little patch of crabgrass, feeling a bit lightheaded from the abrupt movement.

"Now that's a girl!" said Mr. Henderson, and I felt a flit of pride as he positioned the gun against my shoulder, wrapping it with the crook of my arm. "You ever held a gun before?" he asked.

I could smell the beer on his breath. "Yeah," I replied casually, but loud enough for the boys behind me to hear. "Just my dad's revolver," I said, using the name of the gun from a recent episode of *Charlie's Angels*.

"Now all you have to do is aim through here," he said, pointing at the viewfinder, "and pull this trigger here," he said, putting my finger where it needed to go. And I remember feeling a bit nauseous as I willed myself to focus on the tower of cans fifty yards away. But they seemed blurry, and then I heard the rumble of a train in my ears and the echo of a shot and then blackness.

When I came to, Mrs. Henderson was holding a damp washcloth wrapped around ice cubes to what I'd later see was a lump on my temple. Though I tried to walk, Mr. Henderson scooped me up in his sweaty arms and deposited me on a folding chair by the firepit as we waited for my dad to collect me in his pickup truck. Apparently, the bullet was lodged in a weeping willow over by the burn pit.

Who knows if it was heat, hormones, fear, or the recoil that took me down.

"I'm just glad she didn't shoot anybody," I heard my dad tell Mr. Henderson as I awkwardly waved goodbye to my friends, embarrassed to have taken the hoot and holler out of the party just when it was kind of picking up.

CHAPTER TWENTY
White Gloves and Party Manners

I spent much of childhood dreaming of a fairy godmother who, as the grandfather clock in the entry hall chimed midnight, would bibbity-bobbity-boo me into a sparkling gown in a Biltmore-esque mansion where my bedroom would have a walk-in closet filled with Calvin Kleins and Converse. Instead, I kept on living my lowly life under the watchful eye of my frugal mother. So it came as a surprise when Mom signed me up for a somewhat costly Junior Cotillion class when I was thirteen.

"You need to learn social graces," she said. "So if you ever have the chance to go to a ball, you'll know how to dance and which fork to use."

At this point in time, Mom was holding out hope that I would get a full scholarship to Harvard, hobnob with the wealthy, and perhaps become a doctor or—better yet—marry one. She promised me there would be many affluent Princes Charming in these classes and I would do well to learn the ways of their world.

These were the days of Izod shirts in every color, and Add-a-Bead necklaces, pink and green wrap-around skirts, and Reed Hunter Fair Isle sweaters featuring whales or turtles knit around the collars. Preppy boys donned pin-striped Oxford shirts and Ralph Lauren jackets with khaki pants. The wealthy girls from

MacGregor Downs had collections of argyle vests with matching knee socks and carried coordinating monogrammed Pappagallo purses with wooden handles.

My mother took me to Hudson Belk and let me pick out a blue and green plaid jumper. JCPenney had a version of an Izod shirt on sale. Instead of an alligator, it bore a fox over the left nipple and Mom swore that no one could tell the difference. I wasn't totally convinced. But I got one in pale pink, another in yellow, and one in white to go under my jumper. You couldn't beat the savings *or* the variety of looks I could achieve just by changing my shirt.

My private school classmates were from Ravenscroft and Cardinal Gibbons and initially I was intrigued. I'd never held hands with a boy before and there were some attractive options in the class, all sitting in chairs against the wall in a circle around the rec room of a posh North Raleigh community center, not far from the Carolina Country Club. As we were forced to rotate partners, I was going to get the chance to dance with every one of them, whether they liked it or not. With their close-cropped hair and navy-blue blazers, they slumped in their chairs as we waited for our instructor, the matriarchal Nancy Gaddy, to enter the room, at which point all young men were expected to stand and the girls had to sit up straight with gloved hands neatly folded in their laps.

Each class opened with a lecture on etiquette, the importance of Thank You notes, how to make introductions, or how to act in a receiving line. One afternoon when we walked into the room, our circle of chairs was replaced by a long, formally set table, complete with silver candelabras and more utensils than I'd ever encountered, even on the rare evenings when our parents took us out to eat at Neptune's Galley. We learned about salad forks and fish knives, oyster forks and soup spoons, and practiced polite conversation and the proper use of a napkin. The second half of the class was dedicated to learning the dances we were sure to encounter as we waltzed through our lives attending sorority mixers, charity galas and yacht club soirees, none of which I could see in my tea leaves, pinky finger up or not.

When Mrs. Gaddy would call out the foxtrot or the Lindy, boys would scramble across the room to ask a girl to dance. Just like at my junior high school, the playing field was not equal. It was immediately clear who were the cheerleaders and who were the geeks. Mary Hardin Bryan, with her perfect teeth and shiny pennies in her loafers, was always in demand. I was often the last girl asked, and usually reluctantly, after the music had started and the last boy was forced to dodge the swinging elbows of his confident classmates to find me, still sitting in my chair, hands folded neatly, ever hopeful.

When it came time for the Spring Ball, my classmates went to hair salons for fabulous updos, while my mother put my hair in braids and then wrapped them around each other, Princess Leia-style. Those girls all shopped for their dresses at the finest boutiques in Cameron Village, Southern belle ball gowns in a swirl of pale tangerine sorbet or sea foam green. There were crimson Scarlett O'Hara dresses with layers of silken ruffles, and white ball gowns to rival any bride's. They all had elegant white gloves, some to their elbows, others just above the wrist with little buttons down the back.

My gloves were from Kmart's First Communion collection and were a little too small, but they were $4.99 and Mom let me clip off the little yellow flower that adorned each wrist. I kept trying to stretch the fingers, but inevitably they'd bounce back to their true shape, making my hands appear webbed.

My dress was sewn by my mother on her Singer Genie using Simplicity's high-waisted square neckline pattern #3131, long dress version #3. She made it out of a white seersucker fabric and used strawberry-embroidered trim with an eyelet ruffle as the shoulder straps and an accent on the square bodice. She couldn't bear to let the extra eleven and a half inches of trim go to waste so she fashioned a lovely choker out of it with the use of a safety pin.

The week before the Spring Ball, we were given dance cards: 3x4 inch white booklets with *Junior Cotillion 1979* engraved on the cover in swirling gold font with a gold ribbon looped around the corner. The ribbon was provided for girls to tie the dance cards to their wrists. Inside there were ten spaces for the names of the people we would dance with as each number was called.

We spent the first half of our last class discussing the importance of being gracious, asking fellow students that you don't know well, and making sure that everyone in the class had a full dance card for the big event. If, for any reason, there was an empty space on a student's card, Mrs. Gaddy would fill those spaces with students from her advanced classes. It would be a wonderful opportunity, she said, to partner with an exceptional dancer and she recommended leaving one space open for that experience.

It was probably clear to Mrs. Gaddy that I truly hoped to perfect my skills by accepting her challenge in that I still had nine spaces open on my dance card after all the boys had asked the girls in our class to dance. Virtually every spot on my card would need to be filled in by Mrs. Gaddy.

The Cotillion Ball took place at the downtown Civic Center. It was a large affair that brought all of the greater Wake County Junior Cotillion chapters together for an evening of extreme etiquette around ornate punch bowls. White twinkle lights filled potted Ficus trees, and a live orchestra was playing Big Band music as we arrived.

The master of ceremonies walked onto the stage to greet the crowd. He happened to be the long-time anchor of the Channel 5 news and a very familiar face to us all. He was also the husband of our cotillion director, a local celebrity to be sure, and my first brush with stardom. That brush would come a few times too often for me, as my dance card had a series of names that I didn't recognize at all, each written in the careful cursive of Mrs. Gaddy. We were instructed to come to the front of the room by the stage after each dance number was called if we could not locate our partners.

My first dance partner found me fairly quickly. Wade was about 6 foot 3 and I had to reach up to get my hand on his shoulder for the foxtrot. He was in his third year of the program and was actually very kind when I repeatedly stepped on his feet. Perhaps this isn't going to be so bad, I thought. But for the second dance, Strauss' "Lagoon Waltz," the music had easily been playing for over a minute before emcee Charlie Gaddy stepped forward to look at my dance card.

"Brooks Barrington for Suzanne Lowe," he announced into the loudspeaker. "Brooks Barrington, please report to the stage for your second dance."

Reluctantly, a boy I recognized from my class appeared from the shadows. We awkwardly moved one-two-three, two-two-three, both mouthing the count and never meeting each other's eyes.

The third dance of the night was the cha-cha. Again, my partner was not an immediate show. Charlie Gaddy came down off the stage and helped one other young dancer find her partner before gliding up to me, checking my dance card, and calling out, "Blaine Fontaine for Suzanne Lowe."

And so it went throughout the night. Occasionally, my unknown partner would find me and we would foxtrot or waltz in uncomfortable silence, or the master of ceremonies would locate my partner and we would foxtrot or waltz in uncomfortable silence.

At last, the tenth and final dance arrived. In a surprise turn of events, my dance partner did not seek me out.

"Preston Ward," Charlie Gaddy formally announced. "Please come to the dance floor at the front of the hall for the last dance of the evening."

I imagined him a Christopher Atkins look-alike, glimpsing me across the floor and smiling a broad smile as he took my hand in his and twirled me around the Civic Center ballroom. But there was no sign of Preston... or Christopher. Just me, standing by a Ficus tree fairly certain that I'd never even want to go to the kind of parties where this type of dancing or formality was essential, when a hand touched my elbow.

"May I have the honor of this dance?" he asked.

"Sure," I said, surprised as I looked up into his kind eyes and was guided across the dance floor like Cinderella with a certain grace of movement I never knew I had.

Charlie Gaddy looked down at me with a smile and said, "You're an elegant dancer, Suzanne Lowe," as I lay my white-gloved hand in the confident grasp of the television star.

CHAPTER TWENTY-ONE
Bye Bye Broadway

When I was in seventh grade, I developed an aversion to washing my hair and instead covered my head in a bandana to hide the grease, which also resulted in an unfortunate outbreak of acne on my forehead. By eighth grade, my mom had discovered an Avon zit cream that incorporated foundation tint to hide pimples. It made my face look orange and made me even more uncomfortable in my skin. My social life resembled my appearance, spotty and masked.

But by ninth grade, I finally found my tribe and changed the trajectory of my lonely life in the warm embrace of the drama geeks.

East Cary Junior High's drama program was underfunded and taught by a disinterested, mediocre English teacher whom several of my friends referred to as Devil Woman. Russell Barielle and Sean Cloninger would pass her in the hall quietly singing, "She's just a devil woman with evil on her mind…" and when she was out of earshot they'd crescendo, "Beware the devil woman…she's gonna get you!" I always feared there'd be a moment where she'd turn around just in time and actually get them from behind. Sending students to the principal's office was her favorite way to pass the time.

Fortunately for me, one of the drama geeks was also my seventh-grade crush, John Ledford. I still remember him walking into Mr. Smith's algebra class on the first day of school in a red checkered shirt and white painter's pants. I wasn't focused on conjugates and exponential functions and instead tried to catch John's eye across the classroom. As far as I could tell, he never looked my way. But a girl can dream, which is pretty much all I did in Mr. Smith's class until, inevitably, someone would slam a door in the hall or a wise guy would drop a heavy textbook at the back of the class and Mr. Smith would instinctively dive under his desk. Poor Mr. Smith. He had returned from Vietnam about five years earlier and clearly suffered from PTSD. Naturally the class clowns loved to watch him seek cover with their startling antics.

The Devil Woman, Mrs. Martin, instructed us on making silly, stretchy faces while saying "*oooie aaahie ooooh*" and pantomiming animal behaviors rather than what we all really wanted to do, act and perform and step out of our geeky shells to become someone else. We wanted to be stars on the stage since we felt like anything but the stars of our own lives. So when it was announced that we would be putting on a production of *Bye Bye Birdie* that spring, the room went nuts! Though my only singing experience to date was a painful rendition of "Born Free" at the sixth grade talent show, I was cast as Rosie Alvarez, the female lead and long-suffering girlfriend of Albert Peterson, played by none other than my math crush, John Ledford. Our friend Sean was cast as Conrad Birdie, the Army-bound, Elvis-inspired rock star.

When I read the script and discovered that at the end of the musical I'd be engaged to John and I'd get to kiss him, my heart skipped a few awkward beats. Our first kiss was going to be in public, and I was nervous and hopeful that I wouldn't mess up that pivotal part of my personal growth and my development as a leading lady.

While Mrs. Martin provided the scripts and oversaw the casting, she offered little direction in the production. She sent the leads into the piano room to work on our solos alone with no accompaniment, but we goofed off most of the time and when it was my turn to sing, I made up meek excuses about having a sore throat or I left to go to the bathroom. Mine was the role perfected by Chita Rivera on Broadway. She was a fiery Latina and I was a freckle-faced, fourteen-year-old fantasist who had yet to sing a single one of my songs all the way through. Our Conrad Birdie's voice was changing and he struggled to hit the tenor and high baritone notes. By the week of the production, we had run the whole show just twice and merely blocked the song and dance numbers on the makeshift stage in the drama classroom that doubled as the band practice room, with music stands and bongo drums pushed up against the back wall.

On the evening of the big show, folding chairs were lined up in rows in the theatre. Wings were created with chalkboards draped with black bulletin board paper. We got dressed in the adjacent art room.

Conrad was clad in a gold suit and his Adidas were spray-painted gold to match. The backstage scene was chaotic. The gaggle of girls who would soon be vying for Conrad's attention on the mock *Ed Sullivan Show* were warming up for their "We Love You Conrad, Oh Yes We Do" scene as they coated Sean's naturally wavy dark hair in Vaseline to shape it into a smooth teen idol pompadour.

I remember loving the spotlight. I remember the sounds of the folding chairs squeaking on the parquet floor as the audience shifted in their seats. I don't recall forgetting any lines, but I remember my heart pounding before Mrs. Martin played the piano for our barely rehearsed songs. I have little recollection of singing "An English Teacher" or "What Did I Ever See in Him," but I do remember wearing a bright red dress and dancing across the stage with my on-the-spot choreography to "Spanish Rose" in the Shriner's Meeting scene. I remember just going for it in all my unrestrained glory, likely off pitch and knowing I would never sing that song again. I'm sure my heart nearly jumped out of my chest during the kiss scene, but I recall more the anticipation than that actual, unrehearsed first kiss with my crush.

It's been four decades since our one-night run in the East Cary "auditorium" and my memory isn't necessarily clear. There are no photos, nor is there video footage to prove this production ever happened. My mother, who diligently documented nearly every one of my life's milestones with a photo in front of the fireplace, captured no images of me as Rosie and there is no 8mm film that could have been used as a clip on *The Tonight Show* should I ever have made it big on Broadway.

So, I reached out to the critics who were there and have lived to tell the tale. My mom's sister was visiting from New York that weekend. She's eighty-nine now, but her memory of that production remains clear.

"You were so tone deaf," she immediately shares with me. "If I'd not been stuck in the middle of the row and your mother hadn't driven me there, I probably would have left."

She's never been one to mince words. She had a fight with my uncle/her brother many years back and hadn't spoken to him for a decade. When he had a heart attack while on vacation in London, I called her to share the news and she said, "As far as I'm concerned, he's been dead for years." So maybe she wasn't the best person to contact for a charitable review.

I called my dad and it turned out he was one of the reasons for my memory of squeaking chairs. "I just remember squirming in my seat and wishing it was over," he said of his daughter's musical debut.

I found my old crush, John Ledford, and the golden boy, Sean, on Facebook.

"I was never more poorly prepared for a role in all of my life than I was for the part of Conrad Birdie," Sean lamented. He went on to be a lead performer in a rival high school's drama department and did some modeling and theatre work in New York before finding Jesus and leaving the theatrical world that he says has "a sole purpose of pushing the envelope morally, socially and politically." His Facebook posts continue to offer me glimpses into what Trump supporters think.

John said, "I took drama because I was painfully shy. And you should know that was my first kiss and I had a crush on you, as well."

What?! How I'd love to tell thirteen-year-old me that revelation! He's now a marathon runner and former chemistry professor at Houston Baptist University. It has taken us more than three decades and the reach of social media to admit to the mutual adoration of our awkward youth.

And while the original Broadway production received a Tony in 1961, it was not *oohs* and *aahs* but more like lukewarm applause for the East Cary Junior High Drama Department's *Bye Bye Birdie*, but in my heart of hearts, I will always be a fiery, dramatic, captivating Spanish Rose!

CHAPTER TWENTY-TWO
Pins and Needles

I jingle when I walk in my Girl Scout uniform. With dozens of patches, I appear to be the epitome of scouting success, having clearly mastered the arts of cooking, dancing, painting, camping, skating, photography, grilling, first aid and archery among other skills that were signed off on by my distracted mother's free hand while she held her latest offspring on her hip with the other. I may have dabbled in all those patch-worthy things, but I never met any benchmarks for most of them. I think the only arrow I ever shot had a rubber suction-cup tip and I was aiming at my brother's head as I dodged his cap gun bullets. Still, I aimed for the archery patch and somehow was awarded it. My sash was full and jingled with dozens of safety pins, including the ironically pinned-on patch for sewing.

My mother wasn't much of a seamstress either. She regularly mended our pants with patches. When she reattached a button to a shirt, you could feel the knotty lump pressing against your skin. Once, when I was a flower girl in Mom's best friend's wedding, she promised to make a dress that looked just like the one Aunt Lois suggested we purchase from the Sears catalog. Mom made it. It didn't.

When it came to sewing, I was a safety pin-loving fraud, but all I wanted to be was fashionable. I quit Girl Scouts in part because the green uniforms just weren't stylish. Back-to-School shopping was always a disappointment. I'd tear out pages from my *Seventeen* magazines, making vision boards to show Mom the fashion ideas I had in mind when we'd head to the mall, only to have Mom (A) buy me a knock-off brand, or (B) tell me, "That couldn't be hard to make, if you'd learn to sew." It was clear that my mother would never understand my need to dress more like teen models Phoebe Cates and Diane Lane and less like a Sears mannequin.

So, I took matters into my own hands. Literally.

"Where did you get those?" Mom demanded. I was about to leave for school and had pulled together a respectable pink and green preppy ensemble with a kelly-green sweater strategically wrapped over my shoulders to hide the JCPenney fox where the Izod alligator should be, and "S" and "L" stick pins to hold the sweater in place. And they are what Mom was looking at.

I'd begged for them when we were in The Limited the week before. Mom refused. So, when she wasn't looking, I sneakily stuck my initials into the pocket of my not-Jordache jeans.

I was never a good liar. My upper lip quivered, giving away my transgressions. Mom forced me to take off the stick pins and leave them on the kitchen table. After school, she dragged me to the Cary Towne Center and forced me to tell the cashier at The Limited what I had done. With palms sweating, I handed over the tiny pins and admitted the error of my ways as Mom stood behind me smugly enacting judgment like the Great and Powerful Oz.

"Not a big deal," said the teenage clerk nonchalantly as she chomped on a piece of gum.

Mom was furious as I sheepishly slid the pins across the counter.

"We'd like to talk to the manager," demanded my mother. As if giving them back wasn't humiliating enough! Mom was totally trying to bum me out to make her point.

The girl behind the counter with the bright blue eyeliner rolled her eyes as she picked up the phone and mumbled into it then turned to my mother. "She's at lunch. She'll be back in half an hour."

My sister was squirming in her stroller. My mom paced around the racks of corduroys, culottes and plaid flannels. My sister began to cry and Mom, exasperated, grabbed my arm and stormed out of the store. We flew through the mall as she fumed and I was thinking, *Saved by my sister! Saved by the store clerk!*

That is until fifteen minutes later when we pulled into the parking lot of St. Michael's. What was next, the police station? She marched me up to the confessional, opened the door and pushed me in.

Bless me Father for I have sinned. It has been a month since my last confession. I accidentally dropped my baby sister when I was reaching for the phone. She's fine, though. No signs of brain damage. I hid my mushy canned peas in my napkin and, well, I am a thief. I pretend to be something I'm not. I want to be cool and popular and own things that I don't have the money for. If I could sew, I'd design my own clothes, but I can't. I want to be honest and capable, but I'm not. I'm fourteen years old and I hate my mother for not caring about the things that matter to me.

I was assigned my act of contrition. I said my prayers, but I kept on secretly coveting. I moved beyond *Seventeen* to *Vogue* and *Cosmopolitan,* hiding those magazines because of cover articles like the one with Kim Bassinger on it that said *SEX POWER, If You've Got It Flaunt It,* or the one with Paulina Porizkova: *When You Want More Sex Than He Does,* which would have sent my mother into a complete conniption fit and me back to the confessional.

I never told another priest about the lip glosses I tucked into pockets. Or the silk ties that I swiped as gifts for a boyfriend when I temped in the men's department at a local store. The lesson that I learned was more about staying out from under my mom's radar than God's.

CHAPTER TWENTY-THREE
You May Be Right, I May Be Crazy

I jumped out of the car and rushed into the house as soon as we got home from Mass. I flew up the staircase and leaped over my four-poster bed, tuning into WKIX and getting my double cassette deck ready. Casey Kasem's *American Top 40* was underway and I'd probably already missed some coveted songs. I sat on the floor under my window in the two-and-a-half-foot gap between the wall and my bedframe, ready to capture Blondie's "The Tide is High" and Rod Stewart's "Passion," or whatever else I could time just right without Casey talking over the intro. When he did, I'd queue the cassette back up for the next song and hope to get a clean recording of "Hold Me " by Fleetwood Mac. Turns out, "Hold Me " was a *long-distance dedication to Penny in Poughkeepsie.* Apparently, Kevin from Kingston had seen her in the food court and finally got up the nerve to ask her out, but when he turned away to pay for his root beer float, she was gone. I dreamed that one day I'd hear my name in one of those gushy romantic dedications.

The next best thing would be to get a guy to like me enough to give me a mix tape, as if Lionel Ritchie were his personal Cyrano de Bergerac, speaking the truth of a teenage boy's heart. But until somebody found me worthy of "Endless Love," I'd have to make my own mixes.

I borrowed my friend Lori Lee's 8-track of Billy Joel's *The Stranger* when I was in eighth grade and played it incessantly, wishing someone would love me just the way I was. When Mom heard me listening to "Only the Good Die Young," she stormed into the den and told me she never wanted to hear that in her house again, which of course made me listen more closely and consider the Catholic girl's predicament. I already decided I'd rather laugh with the sinners than cry with the saints. "If you're so good," I cursed her under my breath, "well then you're going to die young!" Sadly, she did. But that is another story.

I came home from school one day and *The Stranger* 8-track was unspooled in a tangle of shiny black curls on my bed. Mom vacuumed over my screams. Now I was going to have to buy Lori Lee a new one! And with what money? A $6 album would cost at least three hours of my babysitting income.

Go a little crazy! said the two-page ad in *TV Guide*. I'd seen those Columbia House Record Club commercials on television and the promos in *Tiger Beat* magazine. The reliable face of Dick Clark smiled back, offering up a double music bonus. You could get eleven albums for just a penny! The suggested retail price was $80! What a bargain! I'd dreamily circled my favorites in the tear-out ads for months, but this time I decided to go for it.

First, I had to choose albums, cassettes or 8-tracks. I only had a cassette player in my room, so that made the most sense. But we had a turntable and the Fisher High Fidelity 8-track player downstairs, and I owed Lori Lee *The Stranger* in its original format, so a collection of 8-tracks it was. I felt like a rich person as I carefully chose my music, refining selections over several days, finally deciding on a combination of albums that might make me seem cool like Billy Joel's *The Stranger* for Lori Lee and *Glass Houses* for me; Pat Benatar, Boston, Journey, The Police and Peter Frampton.

Of course, I wasn't thinking of the agreement to purchase eight more selections at regular club prices plus shipping and handling over the next three years when I taped my penny to the postcard and mailed it off to Columbia House.

Once my miracle box arrived, I slowly and strategically added the contents to our family collection, as if 8-tracks were what I was saving all my money for. *Crimes of Passion* landed under the TV cabinet in February and *Zenyatta Mondatta* in April. I gave my mother *Simon & Garfunkel's Greatest Hits* for Mother's Day and *Chicago V* to my father on Father's Day, to quizzical looks. But I was so proud of my generosity and of expanding their musical awareness. Besides, Dad, it was so much better than another Soap on a Rope.

I was only having fun. Wasn't hurting anyone.

Every month, new mailers came with sheets of stamps featuring pictures of album covers. As long as you sent them back saying you didn't want that month's selections, you didn't have to send in any money. I was diligent about intercepting the mail and putting return postcards declining the next orders in neighbors' mailboxes. I didn't have a checkbook yet and I couldn't fathom a way to pay for more records without involving my parents. One month, I somehow missed the postcard and ended up owning Telly Savalas' *Who Loves Ya Baby*.

I couldn't pay for it, so I didn't.

I nearly knocked my mother over one afternoon as I rushed out to the mailbox as the mailman rounded the corner of our cul-de-sac. That likely got Mom's antenna up. The next month an envelope stamped with *Urgent* in red ink lay open on my bed. As I dropped my backpack on my desk and turned around to close my door and ponder my next steps, Mom caught the knob and stood with her arms folded in expectation of my tears and excuses.

"How could you fall for such a scam!" my mother hissed. "And over something as silly as music! You could go to jail, young lady! You're going to have to figure out how to pay for your mistakes and until you do, you're not to come out of this room."

Music wasn't silly. It was my life. It was my escape. But I had only $2.18 in my piggy bank and no babysitting jobs lined up. I decided my only way out was death.

Turn out the light. Don't try to save me.

That night I put on *Dark Side of the Moon* and swallowed a whole bottle of aspirin. I figured that would show them. I woke up in my eyelet-covered canopy bed, soaked in sweat and disappointed that my carefully crafted suicide note had not been discovered. And deeply relieved.

If I'm crazy, then it's true that it's all because of you.

I told my mother I'd use all my Christmas money that year to pay off Columbia House, and that seemed to appease her. I then asked Mom if she'd ever considered suicide.

"Absolutely not," she replied. "God gave me life and only he determines when I die. Why would you ever ask such a thing?"

I pondered my response. *Why?* Because I wondered if anyone would even care or notice my absence, if I had any actual relevance in the world. Because I thought about it almost every day. Because I went to sleep at night dreaming of a funeral for myself like what Tom Sawyer witnessed, and wondered if St. Michael's would be filled, which of my friends would come, if people would cry and what tributes they might share.

"That Suzie was always up to something," my neighbor Joy might say. "She kept the neighborhood on their toes with her Girl's Club activities and potluck parties."

"That kid sure loved the spotlight. If there wasn't a stage for her ideas, she'd make one."

"She sure had a lot of energy!"

"I wish I'd been kinder to her."

"I wish I hadn't yelled at her so much."

"Just think of all the amazing things she'd have done if only she had lived!"

Mom didn't notice the pause in my response about suicide. She went on dusting the furniture, admonishing me about the importance of recognizing God's plan. But I stood there pondering with disbelief someone who'd never even contemplated controlling their own exit from the earth.

As Quarterflash reminded me to *Harden my Heart,* I sobbed into my pillow night after night, my tears a blend of frustration and raging hormones. What I knew for a fact was that I didn't want to live in that house anymore. I didn't belong in a space where you couldn't hide from babies crying, my father yelling, my mother guilt-tripping me into helping ease some part of her stress by doing dishes, vacuuming, or watching my little sisters again. I felt like I was my parents' built-in babysitter, conceived in their twenties so that when they had the kids that they really wanted in their thirties, someone could help raise them. I was a puzzle piece in the family photo with too many soft edges.

It's too late to fight. It's too late to change me.

I intercepted several more threatening letters from the music company over the next few months, and I decided that if Columbia House thought this wasn't my house, maybe they'd leave me alone. I wrote *Moved. No Longer Lives Here. Wrong Address.* on the postcards and envelopes and eventually they stopped coming. Casey Kasem kept reminding me to keep my feet on the ground, but soon this would no longer be my address. I was reaching for the stars.

CHAPTER TWENTY-FOUR
Under the Influence

As far back as I can remember, I had one very specific goal: true love's first kiss. I lived in the little girl fantasyland of glass slippers, poison apples, impossibly high towers, and dramatic rescues by princes charming. I blame Disney movies.

At least I learned the difference between prince and villain at three-years-old when Jeffrey Kniefer stole my Fisher Price lawn mower, hiding it at the entrance to the crawl space under his house. I was stomping my Buster Brown-clad feet in anger when his deceit was discovered. Our mothers told us to "kiss and make up." But this was no fairytale story for me. I punched him in the face.

At Westminster Presbyterian kindergarten, I set my sights on (and my sleeping pad next to) K.R. Holtz. His father was the football coach at NC State University, but I didn't care about sports. I cared about his gap-toothed smile and architectural skills with building blocks. His was the last face I saw as I'd drift off at naptime. He had no idea that he was my first boyfriend, but as Sleeping Beauty taught me, patience is key and true love's first kiss can come after a good long nap.

I sincerely believed that the best way for someone to prove their love was a dramatic rescue and I was also doubling down on "the girl next door" archetype and was determined to get my neighbor Tommy to pay attention to me. When I was eleven and he was twelve, and he was up to bat at the Kenneys' lopsided backyard baseball diamond, he smashed the ball through a forked tree to my spot at third base, nailing me in the forehead. Ever chivalrous, Tommy called "Mom!"

My hero is saving me in my time of need! I thought briefly, until he declared it a foul ball and the boys continued the game while Mrs. Kenney guided me into the house to apply an ice-filled washcloth to the baseball-sized lump forming between my eyes. So much for chivalry!

Snow White had taught me that vanity is not attractive, so in seventh grade social studies, I slumped in my chair uncomprehending how it was that cute guys like Danny Martschenko were so much more interested in the girls who spent half their time rolling Bubble Gum Kissing Potion over their lips while staring at themselves in Maybelline compact mirrors. Sure enough, they'd be kissing jocks by their lockers as soon as the bell rang. When I got my own Bonnie Belle Berry Smash, I stood modestly and lonely by my locker, the only one tasting the berries.

By eighth grade, I'd become desperate for my first kiss. My new friend Michelle was also on the quest. Mom was no fan of our friendship. Initially things were fine.

"I'm going to Michelle's house after school," I would tell my mother in the morning, and I'd get off the bus at the Greenbelt apartment complex just a few stops before my own and head into the bliss that was Michelle's quiet, empty condo where she lived with her single father. At first Mom was happy that I'd stopped asking her to pick me up across town at Giselle's or Julie's. Michelle's was a much more geographically convenient friendship. But when Mom needed to get me for a dentist appointment and I gave her Michelle's address and she pulled up to the row of townhomes nestled in a stand of longleaf pines, Mom started asking questions.

"Will Michelle's mother be there?"

"She doesn't have a mother." I rolled my eyes at the ridiculousness of the question.

"Poor girl. You two should come to our house instead. I don't want you home alone there, and she shouldn't be alone either."

But that was the point. That was what made Michelle so exotic to me. The freedom of her motherless life. The relaxed way that her father trusted her to choose her own snacks and how she got to watch soap operas without questioning the characters' choices. We started saying we were going to the mall after school when really we were curling up on her couch, watching Luke and Laura in the campus disco on *General Hospital* as we gorged on Hostess pudding pies.

So it was surprising when my overprotective mother let me go on a beach trip with Michelle and her father the summer before ninth grade. Michelle's dad had a lady friend who joined us on the second day, so, much like when we were at her house, we were free to roam and hang out at the pier arcade. Michelle had her eye on a Leif Garrett-looking dude with a pronounced Adam's apple who was an ace at Space Invaders. When he laughed, the car keys hanging from a chain off a belt loop on his jeans jangled like sleigh bells. The glow of a cigarette perched between his lips had her mesmerized. We pretended to be looking in our purses for quarters for the Pac-Man machine when Michelle whispered, "Ok, I'm going for it." Michelle was fearless. Maybe because there was no one living at her house to pelt her with promises of penance every time she pushed a boundary.

She grabbed my hand and dragged me with her.

"Hey, can I bum a cigarette?" Michelle asked as if she was a smoker, which she was not. Adam's Apple reached into his pocket and pulled out a crushed pack of Camels. "What's your name?" Michelle asked as the guy we learned was Bobby lit it for her. She looked like a pro as she took a deep drag. I began to wonder what else I didn't know about Michelle.

They talked for all of ten minutes as I absently rolled kissing potion over my lips.

"Want to go for a drive?" Bobby asked, revealing his chipped front tooth.

"Only if Suzanne can come too," responded Michelle.

"Sure," he said. "As long as Marcus can join us."

I hadn't really noticed Bobby's friend Marcus, playing pinball with a mop of brown hair falling across his face. He looked a bit like Potsie from *Happy Days*.

Mom's *"Never get into a car with someone you don't know"* haunted my thoughts but Michelle's *"You only live once!"* won out. Moments later, I found myself in the backseat of Bobby's brown Trans Am, my skin brushing against Marcus' sweaty forearm, a little spark of electricity igniting between us.

Bobby had his arm draped over Michelle's shoulder in the front seat. At the stop light Bobby started French kissing her and the back seat felt way too close to bear witness. But it dawned on me that Marcus could be the Luke to my Laura, the prince to my Cinderella, and tonight might be the night of that first kiss I'd been dreaming of since forever.

Bobby drove to the jetty at the south end of Wrightsville Beach and we walked out to the tip of the barrier island, where the water curves around to meet the channel. Bobby spread a sheet out in the sand for us all to sit on and Michelle and Bobby got right down to business, groping each other under the spotlight of the moon.

"Wanna take a walk?" Marcus finally spoke. In response, I hopped off the sheet like one of those Mexican Jumping Beans my brother gave me for my birthday.

As we walked along the deserted shoreline, I learned that Marcus was from Kernville and was in tenth grade. Apparently that revelation was deep enough to make him comfortable with reaching for my hand. I was sure the quickening of my heart could be heard over the waves. He went on to share that he likes hotdogs and has the highest score in Asteroids amongst his friends, heartfelt confessions that were worthy of a pause in our stroll. He leaned in for a kiss.

Jeepers creepers, this was *it*! My face flushed in the cool breeze as I puckered my lips, but Marcus from Kernville proceeded to part them with his tongue, which totally grossed me out. I tried to stay engaged in this pivotal, life-changing moment, but all I could think about was that he'd clearly had onions on his hotdog earlier in the evening and I could really go for a strawberry slushie right about then. Something cool would feel so much better in my mouth than a sticky, warm, mustard and onion-flavored tongue. Thankfully, Marcus moved away from my mouth and I could breathe again, but he was now focused on my ear and then on my neck, which was nice and tickly, but I nervously giggled then pulled away as his hand began shimmying up under my shirt.

"We should probably get back to our friends," I said. One sloppy kiss was enough of an adventure for one night. And I was worried about Michelle.

When we got back to the blanket, Bobby and Michelle were soaked and laughing, a wave having washed up over them, interrupting their tryst. I was glad to see their wet clothes were still on. Back at the pier parking lot, we said goodbye and Michelle promised Bobby that she'd visit him soon so they could pick up where they left off. I gave Marcus my address and a quick peck on the cheek.

We walked back to the condo laughing about how the sand in Michelle's pockets was a souvenir of her first kiss. Then she spotted my neck. A deep purple bruise was forming. "Looks like you've got a souvenir too!" she said.

When I saw the hickey in the bathroom mirror, I freaked out. We were heading home the next day and no amount of makeup would hide it from my mother. Michelle had the brilliant idea of burning my neck with her curling iron, further branding memories of my first kiss into my skin. Maybe that is what Nazareth meant when they sang "Love Hurts" on the radio.

As Michelle's dad drove us home, we conspiratorially giggled in the backseat, Michelle declaring that she was most definitely in love with Bobby. Every song on the radio took her deeper into her obsession. America's Top 40 was filled with love songs: "Bad Case of Loving You," "I Want You To Want Me" and "Chuck E's In Love." I thought maybe Marcus should mean more to me than he did. But when his letters came, three in that first week, he had no more to say in writing than he did on the beach and shared little beyond his latest Asteroids score, what he had for dinner, and how much he wanted to kiss me again. I thought of that tongue. And I didn't write him back.

Meanwhile, Michelle wrote Bobby a stack of unanswered letters. At thirteen, we didn't find our princes charming, but we remained committed to our quests for the fairy tale ending. I eventually got mine and I hope Michelle did, too.

CHAPTER TWENTY-FIVE
T-Shirt

We make statements about who we are and where we've been through the t-shirts we wear. I currently have a drawer full, declaring me a proud PTA mom who loves National Parks, 5Ks for good causes, Democratic candidates, Fleetwood Mac, Elvis Costello, Hogwarts, and the North Carolina Tar Heels. I've stayed away from poor attempts at comedy with shirts that say "*It Was Me. I Let the Dogs Out*" or "*Straight Outta Burbank.*" My parents taught me to avoid the stupid T, though it was a lesson they never realized they'd given me.

In the spring of ninth grade, just before I turned fifteen, I realized that my wardrobe was lacking. Well, I'd known for years that it lacked the styles that I coveted from the dog-eared pages of fashion magazines, or the Members Only jacket that would attract the likes of AC Musselman, the hunk sitting across from me in social studies class. He looked a lot like my *Tiger Beat* dreamboat Scott Baio, who smiled at me every morning from the poster above my bed. But that April, I realized that *everyone everywhere* who was *anyone* my age had t-shirts with rock bands, cartoon characters, or sayings on them and I didn't have a single one, save for my junior high P.E. shirt featuring the East Cary Imp.

Desperate to be one of the cool kids or at least dress like them, I told my mom about that empty space in my drawer, and perhaps because she knew this was an inexpensive way to appease my incessant but unanswered requests for the latest fashion trends, she agreed that we would go shopping for a t-shirt soon. What I longed for were a few Bert's Surf Shop shirts in bold colors like so many of the popular kids wore over their honeycombed thermal underwear shirts, but I knew there was no way I could get my mother to drive the three hours to Atlantic Beach. I also knew she would never agree to spend money to help someone else promote their business.

"They should be paying us for wearing their names on our bodies, not the other way around!" she lectured.

A few days after my t-shirt request, my mom, little sisters and I walked into Kmart, the antithesis of the trendy surf shop of my dreams, but still, I had hope. Mom hoisted my five-year-old sister into a shopping cart and told me to take the baby in her stroller to check out the t-shirts while she collected the other items on her list. I often enjoyed pretending I was a young mother when I frequently found myself in charge of my youngest sister's stroller in public places. I saw the questioning glances from passers-by, perhaps filled with sympathy or likely disdain at my youthful maternity. So naturally I played it up, saying the kind of things a mother might say to her baby like, "Aren't you my sweet little girl?" and "Do you need mommy to change your diaper?" (That one I actually meant for my mother. I had no interest in changing my sister's diapers.)

I particularly relished when, at the mall on several occasions, my mother would walk up to me while a stranger was complimenting my sister's beautiful blue eyes and would look at my mom and say, "You must be such a proud grandmother." I loved hearing Mom fumble over explanations, appalled at the concept that anyone would even *think* that I might have had sex. And for someone to actually consider that *she* might be old enough to be a grandmother!

Mom was thirty-six.

But it served her right for having me when she was only twenty-one. I knew that she planned it that way so she'd have babysitting when she had her second set of more-loved children later in life, when she'd had more practice and could do her job better. My brother and I were just the guinea pigs.

Back at Kmart, I had selected a few of my favorite shirts and had them spread out across the table next to the stack of navy blue and rust-colored corduroys when my mother walked up with a cart full of diapers and various cleaning products. My middle sister was whimpering about wanting a *My Pretty Pony* and my mother was clearly annoyed.

"Come on, Suzanne," she directed. "We'll come back and figure out this t-shirt business another time." And she wheeled away without even looking at my selection of options with sayings like *Frankie Says Relax* and *Have A Coke and A Smile*. Only I wasn't smiling. I had one mission in going to Kmart that day and I left empty handed.

A week later, I was greeted by the *Happy Birthday* banner my mother had strung at the foot of the stairs adjacent to the kitchen where she always hailed our birthdays with balloons scotch-taped to the chandelier and the same pink and white streamers dotted with masking tape from a decade of her three daughters' birthdays crisscrossing the room like octopus arms, stretching from the range hood to the salad bowl atop the fridge, from the hutch to the pantry molding. Mom stood by the sink smiling and said what she always said on the birthday mornings, "Does it feel any different to wake up and be *fifteen*, Suzie Sunshine?"

Each birthday, family gifts were piled up on the table in front of our seat along with a box of "birthday cereal." Mom wouldn't let us have sugarcoated cereal any other time of year, but on our birthdays, we could pick out anything we wanted from the cereal aisle. I could count on my brother to guarantee me one annual bowl of Lucky Charms and I always ensured he got one annual bowl of Golden Grahams.

I tore through my gifts on this Memorial Day Monday: a stuffed animal from my sisters, a push-button phone for my room from my father, who worked for Southern Bell and knew how to connect the line upstairs. This was a big *score* because our downstairs phone was still rotary. I'd not only gained privacy, I now had quick-dial convenience! My brother gave me a handmade card promising to let me watch *General Hospital* for the next week even though it came on at the same time as *The Flintstones*, which often resulted in epic family room battles.

The last package contained two brand new t-shirts! Finally, I thought, I too can make a statement as I walk the junior high school halls! One was lemon yellow with a rainbow arching over the words *Smile, God Loves You*. The second shirt was gray and imprinted with black lettering that stated *I've Got What It Takes But Nobody Wants It*.

Mom laughed at the look on my face. She thought it was funny and that she was so clever. But she clearly didn't get it. *At all*. How a prude like my mother would give her daughter such a billboard to wear across her slowly developing chest, I'll never understand. And I was oblivious, too. I didn't get why I received so many catcalls and inappropriate comments when I wore it. I welcomed the attention likely because I didn't comprehend it. And my mother, who didn't want me mistaken for the mother of her youngest daughter, was naively oblivious to how what she thought was a silly t-shirt would be interpreted in the world. Eventually, I got grossed out by solicitous offers from strangers to take what I've got. The birthday gift became a nightshirt before making its way into the ragbag.

That fall, my father spent three months working on a job in Fort Lauderdale, Florida.

"Get me a t-shirt while you're there!" I declared while lying in my canopy bed, talking on my push-pad phone. I'd imagined a cool shirt from an exotic Floridian surf shop.

When Dad got home, he proudly presented me with a bright red Tee from a barbeque joint he frequented down the street from his hotel. Apparently, he also failed to understand the impact words on a t-shirt might have on the teenage daughter wearing it. Over the front left breast in white letters, my present from daddy said *Munch On My Ribs.*

CHAPTER TWENTY-SIX
Thanks For Life, Mom

I t's Mother's Day, 1979. We're up for the early morning Mass because afterwards we're heading to the governor's mansion to drop off blood-red roses. Mom has a bucket full in the back of the Ford LTD. We'll leave the windows of the car cracked while we're in church so the flowers don't wilt before we can give them to people gathered in front of the wrought-iron gates.

"Governor Jim Hunt is a dirty Democrat," Mom says. "He doesn't care about the babies." She pins a pink button to my dress and a blue one to my little brother's suit jacket. *Thanks For Life, Mom* they read.

We pull into the parking lot at Sacred Heart Cathedral, a heavy drizzle coming down from thick gray clouds. My brother kicks at the gravel as we walk around the back of the car where a neon yellow bumper sticker reminds us that *Abortion Stops a Beating Heart.* Images of helpless embryos in fetal sacs frame the message. Father Bill echoes Mom's sentiments in his homily as he speaks on the sanctity of human life. I can't possibly counter-protest. Of course, all babies deserve a chance to grow inside their mothers safely. I am twelve and I do not have the slightest idea where babies come from. Don't ask. Don't tell. It's the mantra in my house. And I am totally against *murder*!

The sun is out when we leave Mass—a sign from God of our righteous work, Mom assures us. Guards stand by the gates to the governor's mansion and we pass out our roses, one representing each of the babies needlessly murdered in the state of North Carolina that year. Jesse Helms prepares to take the podium. The crowd is dotted with nuns and people carrying signs reminding us that *"Abortion is not a right, it's a wrong."* Across the street, the hippies have their signs, too. They want the right to kill babies.

The following year, I'm in junior high and desperate to join my friends at the State Fair. As we drive down Blue Ridge Road, you can see the red and white big top going up and the metal arms of the Spider and Tilt-A-Whirl coming together. The smell of the livestock and petting zoo will soon mingle with the sweet scents of Carolina BBQ, ham biscuits and deep-fried dough.

But Mom says the only way I can go is if I put in a minimum of ten hours at the Wake County Right to Life booth to secure a free volunteer pass. So I stand at the table with the life-size resin replicas of fetuses from nine weeks gestation to full term. I share the doctrine I'd learned while I pass out brochures depicting slimy babies carelessly tossed in metal trashcans.

We speak of saving the babies, but never of where they come from. My understanding of the birds and the bees exists under a thick blanket of secrecy in the house of my childhood.

When I am ten or so, I ask my mother "What is sex?"

She responds, "All you need to know is to check the box that says female." Her pursed lips put a halt to any future questions.

In the nick of time, the week before my thirteenth birthday, Mom hands me a small booklet with a plain, pale blue cover with the title *A Doctor Talks to 9-to-12-year-olds* written by a doctor and a priest. In it I learn about how parents' love can create new life. The paragraph about intercourse is brief. I'm left with many questions and no one to talk to about them.

The three-paragraph "chapter" about "Changing Interests and Feelings About Sex" focuses mostly on young children getting their messages about loving and understanding right from wrong in Bible School. The teen section centers on girls learning how to be a wife and making a comfortable home before being ready to become a mother. I am so confused about what I feel when I think about handsome Chris Harrison from Social Studies class as I try to get to sleep on those balmy spring nights.

And then there is page sixty-five. The title of this chapter is "A Bothersome Question." The authors of my only source for sexual education up to that point go on to explain:

> *Boys and girls may have heard that masturbation causes illness, or pimples, or insanity, or a boy may fear that it will use up all his semen so that he cannot become a father when he is grown. For centuries such beliefs were accepted, but physicians today assure us that none of these things is true. Perhaps the greatest harm is the guilt and fear that most young people feel if they masturbate...It **is** possible that excessive masturbation is a warning that the boy or girl takes so much satisfaction in his own body that he doesn't develop friendships easily, especially with the other sex. Such a young person should speak with some older person who he trusts to find out how he can make more friends and develop more constructive interest in life.*

In seventh grade, my mother reluctantly agrees to sign a paper allowing me to participate in the public school's sexual education program.

"Well with those Democratic crazies in office, Lord knows what they will allow teachers to subject our students' young minds to," she mutters as I quickly stuff the permission slip in my backpack before she changes her mind. *Finally*, I am going to get some real, useful information!

Mrs. Trent's classroom is covered with posters of the Voyager spacecraft and Spacelab, with planet mobiles made by students hanging from the ceiling. She goes deep into details about the atmosphere on the planets, and we can count on her to take off on tangents about whether there really might be Martians on Mars or whether those women in Kentucky were *really* abducted by UFOs. But the sperm and the egg and the fertilization part is exactly like in the doctor's booklet. It isn't until the last day of our chapter on sexuality that it looks like we might finally be getting to the truth about exactly what sex is.

I don't recall what we are told, but clearly, I still don't get it. My journal at the time states in big, bold letters: *Today Mrs. Trent told us all about SEXUAL INTERSECTION!*

When I get my period at fourteen, I know I'm not dying thanks to Judy Blume's *Are You There God? Its Me, Margaret.* Unfortunately, though, the first time it happens, we are at Grandma Rose's stuffy little house in Elizabethton, Tennessee, at the foot of Lynn Mountain with its giant sign that says *JESUS SAVES* in huge red block letters. I can't tell my grandmother. My father's mother is a Southern Baptist and something about that sign makes me feel like I'm too soiled for saving. I can't tell my mother. Surely, she'll make a scene and rush me out the door to the Dollar Store across from Taco John's for Kotex pads.

I fold up a washcloth and stuff it in my underpants and walk bowlegged for the remainder of the trip, and I sit uncomfortably on my wad of terrycloth for the six-hour ride home to Raleigh. At some point Grandma must have noticed her washcloth supply had greatly diminished following our visit. Meanwhile, I have a Wonder Bread bag full of rags that I stuff into a McDonald's Happy Meal box and bury in the trashcan by the side of our house. I even offer to take my brother's job of scooping up the dog poop and dump it on top of the trash pile to further ensure my private plight won't become knowledge.

Shame and secrecy mark my journey to womanhood.

"You are not to use tampons until you are married," hisses my mother in the feminine protection aisle at Piggly Wiggly.

"But Mom, the boys can see my maxi pad in my PE shorts," I whisper, desperate to convey the urgency of this issue.

"Well then I'll give you a note to get out of class," she offers.

"But I can't skip gym for one week every month," I say.

"Girls do it all the time," says Mom. "Be grateful you don't have to wear belts with pads like I did and stop complaining. You have a good forty more years of this so get used to it."

Then she threatens me with Toxic Shock Syndrome. A virtual certainty, she says. "Use one of those forbidden wads of cotton and you'll wake up to a rash all over your body and just as you call for help, you'll have a seizure and it will be too late."

I am destined to be a rebel and decide toxicity is worth the risk. I march up the street to Little Sue's Mini Market with the $4 I earned chasing the Sutton twins around their split-level house for two miserable hours and buy a box of tampons. I hide the box behind my Nancy Drew books. *The Mystery at Lilac Inn* and *The Quest of the Missing Map* serve as a blockade for *The Secret of the Hidden Tampax Box*, which my mother finds one day while "dusting" my room, which means she was really looking for clues in my diary. I come home from school to find a blizzard of feminine protection with wrappers, cardboard applicators and cotton inserts shredded around my room.

"What the heck!" I scream down the stairs.

"You clean up that mess before dinner," she yells back. "That'll teach you not to defy my rules while you're living under my roof, young lady!"

She's sure I'll learn my lesson in wastefully spending my hard-earned babysitting dollars, but I only become stealthier in my storage, and more determined to keep my life's personal journey to myself.

CHAPTER TWENTY-SEVEN

Cheerleader

Down the halls of my junior high school, they paraded like royalty with a confidence I could only dream about, proudly wearing their short, pleated white skirts and sweater vests with green trim, pom-poms spilling out of lockers plastered with the faces of John Stamos, Ralph Macchio and Matt Dillon, while East Cary's pubescent versions of those heartthrobs in flannel shirts and letter jackets hung on their every word. I'd stand at my locker, with *Teen Beat* tear-outs of Shaun Cassidy and Parker Stevenson grinning back, and longingly look on in my peripheral vision, doing everything not to draw attention to myself. I didn't have the right to talk to them, me with my off-brand jeans and wooden Add-a-Beads.

I wanted desperately to be a cheerleader. It was my ultimate dream of success, an earned spotlight that could change the trajectory of my loser life. When I babysat for the Velascos, after I put Angelique and Gabriel to bed, I'd sit down with their mother Jacque's old high school yearbook. Jacque O'Neill was a beautiful, bubbly blonde, poodle-skirted cheerleader and homecoming queen. Clearly the golden girl at her school, and the most beautiful mom on the block now. That was what I wanted for my own future. But it seemed impossible in the confines of the life I was currently leading.

When I learned that I'd be going to the new high school alongside maybe only a dozen kids from my junior high, I saw an opportunity. I could start over. No one there would know I was a geek. I began brightening my aura with Sun In and decided I would try out for cheerleading. When all those stuck-up popular girls from Cary High heard—or better yet, saw—me on the sidelines at cross-town rivalry games, they'd realize they had miscalculated this nerd. I was as cool as they were, just more understated about it.

Tryouts required us to learn dance routines and jumps like pikes, herkies and hurdlers. Though I tried repeatedly to get air on the braided rug in our den, I never got anywhere near the cottage cheese ceiling. For weeks, I attempted to perfect my cartwheels in the crabgrass under the clothesline, where Mom still hung out my underwear in full view of the five now mostly teenaged Kenney boys who lived next door. We begged our mother to use the dryer, but she said it was a waste of electricity. So there, for all to see, hung my bras and panties, also untouched by tuck jumps when I practiced in the grass. My cartwheels resembled crab legs more than starfish.

But I did have one thing going for me. I was spunky and full of spirit. Why, Spunk and Spirit were practically my middle names! As a kid, I'd try anything and perhaps falsely believed I was actually good at it. After ballet recitals, I knew I could choreograph the dances better than my teacher and I would definitely have chosen better costumes. I loved poring through the catalogues in the lobby of the dance studio as I'd wait for Mom to pick me up. It never made sense to me why most of our costumes only had basic lines of sequins and plain tutus. I wasn't paying any attention to the price charts in the back. After the shows, I'd create programs for the studio I imagined I'd one day have in my off hours when I wasn't working at my veterinary clinic. I'd name the dances Cinnamon Dreams and Waltz of the Daisies and select the songs they'd be performed to. I'd get out colored pencils and markers and design all the elaborate costumes and then begin the choreography. I was a confident dreamer back then. But by the time I got to junior high, I'd started tamping down those qualities, wanting more to be noticed as a budding beauty than for my straight As and creativity.

Once I became a cheerleader, though, I just knew that my joyful, spunky self would reemerge. I could choreograph both my life's trajectory and dance routines for my team.

However, my herkies did not get higher. My cartwheels never got better. I had never taken a gymnastics class and never thought to ask for help. I likely made it to the finals because my commitment to the cause outshined my lack of skill. I made it as far as the final two before I was cut as an incoming sophomore. I tried again as a junior, though I'd done no extra work to improve my skills. Again, I made it to the finals, but I didn't get picked. I thought my senior year would be a sure thing, that they'd see just how much I wanted this and what an asset I'd be to the team. I was the Pep Club president, after all. Again, I made it to the finals, but I didn't get picked.

I was totally bummed out. I would never be the Queen Jacque of my yearbook. My dream was a bust. But I thought, what would young Suzie do? She would design her own opportunity.

My high school had a jaguar mascot. My friend Nancy had played the role her senior year, wearing a tired old matted animal-printed, footed pajama-type uniform. But Nancy was graduating. What if we could reimagine the mascot? What if there were two of us? I talked my best friend, Cathy, into pitching the idea to the cheerleading coach and I got out my colored pencils and sketched a design for a jaguar-print, short-skirted cheerleading uniform complete with a tail and pinned-on ears. Remarkably, the coach agreed.

And so we found ourselves at NC State University's cheerleading camp. We choreographed our own mascot routine to

"Stray Cat Strut" and relished the attention garnered by the sexy cat costumes. We clearly pissed off several of the cheerleaders when we were both nominated for the homecoming court. So pissed off were a couple of them that—during halftime of the big game, when we were set to walk onto the football field wearing our giant white chrysanthemum corsages with the orange pipe cleaner As for Athens in the center, arms intertwined with our escorts—someone set off a smoke bomb that filled the field with a thick fog. All of the photos in the yearbook were blurry, thus shattering my Jacque O dreams.

Truth was, I didn't even know much about the sports I would have been cheering for. It wasn't until I realized that being able to call out "That's palming!" or "He has no points in the paint!" while watching a basketball game or shouting "Unnecessary roughness!" during the NFL playoffs could score points with a potential love interest that I finally started paying attention and shaking my pom-poms with purpose.

CHAPTER TWENTY-EIGHT
Golden Girl

I look like a ghost and have the eucalyptus scent of a koala habitat with Noxzema masking my face. I am miserable. I kissed Shane Walsh in the dugout and haven't heard from him since. Meanwhile, I saw Angela Holland and Suzanne Hawkins walking through the food court at the Cary Towne Center when I was coming out of Contempo Casuals with my mother. I took a few steps back, distancing myself from Mom's fat pregnant belly as she pushed my sister in the stroller. All the cute guys from junior high were seductively slurping their Orange Juliuses while checking out my dream girls with their fabulously feathered hair, shirts falling off their shoulders like Jennifer Beals in *Flashdance*, and nothing coming between them and their Calvins. When Angela and Suzanne dressed up as mice and sang Peaches and Herb's "Reunited" at the eighth grade talent show, I knew the only thing that would have made their act better was if the duet were a trio and I'd been invited to be the third mouse.

But here in my bedroom on a Saturday night, I am sure those mice and all the cute boys who love them are out at a party somewhere while I sit under my checkered canopy, deep-cleaning my pores. I am bummed out to the max. How can I make myself more desirable? What is the key to having fun? I am flipping through *Seventeen* magazine when the answer stares back like a magical revelation, shimmering under the spotlight of my Holly Hobbie lamp. *Where the boys are!* says the caption, with a picture of a good-looking man staring adoringly at a sexy blonde. The paragraph below says *Just spray on Sun In under the sun and see what happens. To your hair, maybe even to your life.*

Why, *that* is the logical answer! Amy and Heather are blonde. Blondes have more fun. Therefore, if I am no longer a straggly brunette, I, too, could have fun. And turn heads. And have friends. And go to parties. And be happy. Be a Peaches and Herb mouse.

The next day I go to Kerr Drugs and buy a bottle of *Super Sun In* with my babysitting bucks. I don't do a test patch. Oh no, I spray it all over my head and sit in the lawn chair in the sunniest part of our yard and wait for the metamorphosis to begin. I imagine that when I start high school the next year, I will be blonde and beautiful, and at the top of the social hierarchy alongside the quarterback, the cheerleaders, the class president and the girls with Pappagallo purses.

Day one. I shower and dry my hair. I stare this way and that in the mirror. It might be a little lighter.

Day two. I tell my friend Giselle that I cannot go to Skate Town for the 50 percent-off afternoon skate. Yes, it would be cooler in the air-conditioned rink, but it is too dark in there. Instead, I sit in the sun on a 98-degree day with 110 percent humidity, my hair crunchy with peroxide, lemon juice and silk amino acids. You must pay a price for beauty, I reason, and I am willing to empty my piggy bank for the cause. That night, as I dry my hair, my true self begins to emerge. Day three and day four, I am becoming a golden girl. Those high school boys are not going to know what hit them.

Thing is, the grass isn't always greener.
It's often Astroturf when you look up-close.

A vicious cycle soon occurs. Hair grows, roots reveal themselves. Sun In oxidation dries out hair and my once thick locks
become brittle. They look a bit orange. And after a summer
vacation at a dingy beach motel with a pool that is four parts
chlorine to one part water, my hair turns green. When I finally
get the color right, I decide what will really make me pretty is
curly blonde hair, so I get a perm.

Mrs. Richman, Mom's friend who went to beauty school but
has not worked in a beauty parlor for at least a dozen years,
comes over with her pink terry cloth towel with the head hole
and a box of coordinating pin-curl rollers and a mixing bowl.
Mom opens all the kitchen windows so the skunk and sulfur
smell doesn't kill us all. Years later, if you scratch-and-sniffed
the goldenrod floral wallpaper in our kitchen, you'd surely have
gotten whiffs of Toni Silkwave, Mom's beloved and everyone
else's hated chicken livers and onions, Daddy's Prince Albert
pipe tobacco that wafted in from the back porch, and the rubber
cement used on countless school projects at the kitchen table.

My perm kills whatever bouncing or behaving my Pert sham-
poo promises, and I am left with yellow straw, but the boys do
seem to notice me. Upperclassmen ask me out. Tenth grade feels
like a miracle transformation. The girl who so often hid in the
bathroom during slow dances in junior high is the first on and
the last to leave the high school gym dance floor after every home
football game. I feel like proof that blondes have more fun.

I not only color my hair, I color my perception of what is
important in life. Boys hold more value than books. A grade A
in kissing is more worthwhile than straight As on a report card.
My goody two-shoes ninth grade image dissolves into a Sam
Goody-obsessed, Candies shoe-wearing, proud-to-come-off-as-
an-airhead-even-though-I-was-said-to-be-gifted-and-talented girl.
The only gifts and talents I want are popularity and a boyfriend.

Nearly five decades have gone by since I first saw that ad that changed my life's trajectory. We do not know what color my hair might be today had I not turned toward the sun. Perhaps, had I stayed the "dirty blonde" my hairdresser now calls the natural color at the base of my neck, I'd have taken physics in high school and not adopted the dumb blonde persona that I consciously morphed into. I got a D in chemistry the next year and I was both gutted and proud of my ability to evolve. My unformed brain determined that impossibly tight jeans and irrationally yellow hair were the gateway to happiness. I think my Jordaches cut off some of the air supply to my brain.

And speaking of Air Supply. I am often "Lost in Love…then back on my feet and eager to be what you wanted."

I am like a chameleon, changing more than just my hair for whatever boy with whom I am trying to inspire a love match. If Tom likes baseball, I become the biggest baseball fan he's ever known, borrowing my brother's binder of baseball cards and memorizing a handful of seemingly relevant stats. In 1982, I can cite for you the greatest successes by George Brett, Nolan Ryan, Rod Carew.

If Kirk loves Rush and The Who, well, I am the biggest lover of Geddy Lee and Pete Townsend that you've ever seen. The only time this pays off is when I date our eventual valedictorian and return to getting straight As my senior year, which is likely how I demonstrate my potential on my transcript and get into a decent college.

Sun In is the gateway drug to fake tans and fake lashes, colored contacts and other DIY beauty. The quest for a more perfect blonde, and thereby a more perfect life, leads to many interesting choices in the Clairol aisle. Ash Blonde can appear pale green. There is nothing neutral about Gold Neutral blonde when it turns orange. Don't swim with Ultra Cool blonde hair if you actually want to be cool.

Under my crown of gold, who I am is a big question mark. What is real? I write my memoir in a quest to reunite with the girl I used to be so that I can more authentically embrace the woman I am.

CHAPTER TWENTY-NINE
Flashlight

For my confirmation in tenth grade, I wore a high-collared, lacy Gunne Sax dress and I agreed to all of the professions of faith in the Nicene Creed, even though I was twisted and knotted with unanswered questions.

The following week, for some reason, I thought it might be a nice variation to my normal jeans-and-a-sweater ensemble to wear my virginal *Little House on the Prairie* church dress to school. There I was, reeking with Love's Baby Soft "because Innocence is sexier than you think" while I sat in civics class all prim and proper with my hair in a bun. I had Emily Post posture, well-earned under Mom's command that I walk around the house and up and down the stairs balancing a dictionary on my head.

Civics was like a dulled-down episode of *School House Rock* with Mr. Wilson in his sweater vests droning on and on about bills on Capitol Hill, the three-ring government and the great American melting pot. Anyone who aced the test on the preamble to the Constitution did so by singing the song from the cartoon and not because of anything Mr. Wilson said.

When the bell rang and I was leaving class, Kerry Watson, a black guy who'd been sitting behind me all year, put his hand on my shoulder and whispered in my ear, "I'm going to tie my sweatshirt around your waist and walk with you to the nurse's office." *What the heck was he talking about?* "Just trust me."

Now Kerry and I had always been friendly, but I didn't know him. It wasn't until I got to the bathroom in the office that I realized the mortification this guy saved me from.

A giant blood stain that no amount of Clorox could ever fully get out had destroyed my frilly Gunne Sax dress on its second wearing. Mom was going to be furious. I spent the rest of the day wearing gym clothes with my white espadrilles. But Kerry and I were forever connected by his kindness.

When I got home, Mom set out to save the dress with peroxide and baking soda to no avail.

"You should have saved it for a special occasion," she grumbled.

"Well, you should have let me wear tampons!" I yelled as I slammed my door in embarrassment. I was using tampons but had no idea how often to change them and no one to ask, considering that my mother had forbidden their use until marriage.

A couple months later, Kerry wanted to enter the school talent show with a dance number he was choreographing to Michael Jackson's "Beat It." He asked me to be one of the dancers. I'd do anything for Kerry, so yes, of course I agreed. "*You wanna stay alive, better do what you can, so beat it, just beat it,*" Michael warned, and like characters in *West Side Story* we rehearsed hip-gyrations, side-slides and moonwalk moves and Kerry ate up the spotlight, nailing the role of ringleader, surrounded by his gang of mostly girls.

Meanwhile some of the coolest guys in school were in a band called *Twilight of the Dude Gods* and they were jamming hard to this amazing song they introduced as "Radar Love." At rehearsal I got gutsy and walked up to the handsome lead singer, Lars, and said "That song is amazing! You guys need a record deal!" I had no idea a Dutch band called Golden Earring had already done that. In 1973. Hot Lars, a senior, rolled his eyes.

But later, when some of their cables got disconnected from the amp and Lars called out, "Does anyone have a flashlight?" Why yes, I did. I'd brought one from the house, along with a roll of duct tape, just in case.

When I got home from rehearsal, my mom asked me if I had the flashlight.

"No, but I'll get it at the talent show tomorrow. Promise."

But I forgot.

When I left for school the next day, she said, "Make sure to ask that Lars boy about the flashlight. It has rechargeable batteries and those are expensive."

But I forgot.

On the last day of tenth grade, as I left the house, Mom said, "That Lars boy is graduating. Get his address and we can go by this summer and get our flashlight." Well, that would be awkward. I didn't do it.

Periodically throughout high school, Mom asked me if I could ask Lars' younger brother Mark, the guitarist in *Twilight of the Dude Gods,* if he still had our flashlight, but that would be so weird and embarrassing. So, I didn't do it.

Time flies and bands break up.

Flashlights lose their juice.

Friends lose touch.

People die.

By our tenth high school reunion, as I was leaving the house, my mother said, "Do you think that Simonsen boy will be there?"

"Gosh, Mom, probably, but I don't know."

"Well, if he is, ask him if he happens to know where our flashlight is. Rechargeable batteries are expensive."

Mark was there, and I didn't bring up the flashlight this time either. But Kerry Watson wasn't at the reunion. When the DJ played "Beat It," some of us reprised a few of the moves from the talent show in his memory. Kerry was the first person I personally knew to lose his life to the devastating AIDS epidemic that ravaged the gay community in the 1980s. We'd hardly heard about it as we headed out into the world in 1984, but by the end of the decade, it was the second leading cause of death among men aged twenty-five to forty-four. It had never dawned on me in high school that Kerry was gay. The gentle boy with the sweatshirt. The choreographer. I guess it was obvious to some, but it never crossed my mind. Kerry had shined a light with his kindness and his memory beats on.

CHAPTER THIRTY

Good Girl Gone Somewhat Bad

S ometimes parents have a way of surprising us. Just when you think you know what they're going to do, BAM! They don't do it. My mom was predictably cautious, often neurotic and always guided by Catholicism. She was sure that *Houses of the Holy* was satanic, so naturally I played my Led Zeppelin album at full volume.

In junior high school, loud music and tampons were about the extent of my rebellion, but when I started high school in 1981, I was determined to shake the geeky image that plagued me in junior high. Fortunately for me, I had the perfect opportunity to do it as one of only a handful of students from my ninth grade class that were heading to the newest high school in Raleigh.

Up to that point, I'd been quite sheltered. I was rarely allowed to go to parties where there were boys, except for the junior high dances where my friends and I would cluster together in the middle of the cafeteria dancing to Kool and the Gang's "Celebration." But when Air Supply's "All Out Of Love" would come on, the dance floor would clear, revealing only couples swaying back and forth, the popular girls all spritzed with Love's Baby Soft, their shimmering smiles coated in Bonnie Belle lip gloss, and the boys in their pin-striped shirts smelling of their dad's Drakkar Noir. I'd slink off to the bathroom so as not to get pegged as a dorky wallflower. My fantasy was to someday be on that dance floor in the arms of a lanky dreamboat under the disco ball while Styx crooned, "You know it's you babe, giving me the courage and the strength I need..."

As much as I needed someone to dance with, I also needed courage and strength to navigate the minefield at home. You see, my mother had a tendency toward overreaction, from the Tampax blizzard of 1980 when she found my hidden box and tore the tampons to shreds to make the point that I was forbidden to use them to the time she called all of my junior high school friends' mothers after reading their daughters' messages in my yearbook.

I'd hardly read any of the entries myself when Mom got hold of it.

"Do you know what our girls are up to?" my mom asked Giselle's mother. "Have you seen the *awful* things written in their yearbooks?"

One friend had written, *It's been pretty wild raisin' hell in Miss Hill's class with you!* Miss Hill was the physical education and health teacher who never shaved her legs. When she wasn't yelling, she spoke in "whistle": the silver metal piece was nearly always in her mouth and she'd blow it for every real or perceived infraction, even in health class. I am quite sure the only hell I raised in that class was when I whispered with my friends while being benched during kickball or dreaded dodgeball games. Any giggles were abruptly silenced by the shrill and threatening whistle.

A boy I don't even remember knowing wrote, *It was pretty great last night. Hope we can do it again. What are we going to name the kid?* At that point in my life, I'd experienced only a couple sloppy kisses and I'd yet to sprout breasts, though not for a lack of trying. If my mother had bothered cross-referencing his class photo, I'm sure she'd have realized it was a ridiculous attempt at a joke from someone I hardly ever talked to.

One of my best friends wrote, *We're going to get wasted all summer long!* Several people scribbled, *Don't party too hard this summer!* The truth was, I hadn't partied at all at that point in my life, so I guess I figured if I was going to get into trouble for it anyway, I may as well just do it.

One of my best friends wrote *COCKtail* so big it filled a page, and she used different colored sparkly markers to write inside the bubbled letters of *COCK: Forgery! Joy Jelly! Motion Lotion! Bum Scene!* and *Finger Applicator!* My mother didn't know what to make of that so she grounded me.

"Words have consequences," Mom said.

"But I didn't write any of that!" I countered.

"Well, you better hope I don't ever see what you wrote," she replied.

I served my sentence in my room blaring Stevie Nicks' "Edge of Seventeen" and wishing I was seventeen, or better yet eighteen, so I could get the heck out of there.

Once paroled, I spent most of that summer on my friend Lori Lee's Juliet balcony overlooking Walnut Street, smoking cigarettes and polishing off the airplane bottles of whiskey and vodka her father brought home from business trips and reading a book called *Dirty Little Limericks*, with fine, memorable poetry like:

> *There was a young sailor from Brighton*
> *Who remarked to his girl, "You're a tight one."*
> *She replied, "'Pon my soul,*
> *You're in the wrong hole;*
> *There's plenty of room in the right one."*

Oh, we thought we were so daring, giggling over risqué limericks, letting the f-bombs roll off our tongues, giddy on fifty milliliters of Smirnoff.

Oddly, my sheltered life seemed to have an expiration date. All through junior high, when I would ask, "When can I...?" (Insert: Go on a date? Ride in a car with a boy? Get my ears pierced?) my mother would say, "When you're in high school."

Suddenly I *was* in high school and the world opened up to me, only I wasn't at all prepared. We'd never discussed the reasoning behind the rules and now they were essentially gone. No one ever talked to me about not getting into cars with people who'd been drinking. It is a miracle I survived to tell the tale.

As part of my personal renaissance, I gathered the courage to run for class office. I still cannot believe my mother and the school administration allowed me to use my campaign slogan. My last name was Lowe and my tempera-painted signs declared: *GET HIGH VOTE LOWE!* Not surprisingly, I won the elections all three years. My platform had nothing to do with legalizing pot. Surely no one living in RJ Reynolds tobacco land in the 1980s would believe that by the 20-teens you couldn't smoke cigarettes in most places, but that pot is prolific and legal in much of the country.

My once omnipresent mother didn't seem to notice my wild behavior, busy as she was with an infant and a toddler at home. The decline in my grades was likely attributed to the transition to high school. I still had a curfew, but when I would stumble into the house way past 11 p.m., I'd set the clock back, pop in a breath mint, and wake my dad, who was usually asleep on the couch. I'd whisper, "I'm home," and point to the clock which read 10:55 p.m., even though it was often actually one or two in the morning.

Around that time, my father took that temporary job in Fort Lauderdale, Florida, where he got me that *Munch on My Ribs* t-shirt. Our family had discussed the possibility of moving and decided it wouldn't be a good idea to uproot my brother and me from our schools, so Dad agreed to take the job for just four months, giving his company time to find a permanent replacement. This was not a good time for "The Hammer" to leave his increasingly wayward teenage daughter.

Always eager to test the waters, one afternoon when my mother was vacuuming in the den, I lit a cigarette in the kitchen. Within moments, the whir of the vacuum ceased and my mother was standing in front of me.

"What do you think you're doing?" she asked through clenched teeth.

"I'm smoking. What does it look like?" I replied like the rude little shit I was becoming.

She looked at me angrily at first and then she said, "Can I have one?" effectively taking the wind right out of my inflated fifteen-year-old sails.

"Uh, ok."

And we sat at the kitchen table smoking our cigarettes. Though we were living amidst tobacco fields where Marlboro Man billboards lined the highways from the Outer Banks to the Smoky Mountains and there were designated "smoking flats" for teachers *and* students at our school, *no one ever smoked at our house.* My dad had a collection of pipes with all sorts of flavored tobaccos, but he was only authorized to use them out by the shed in the backyard.

But there I sat with my mother as she told me about how she smoked as a teenager in Brooklyn. How, even though doctors weren't saying it was bad for pregnant women yet, when she found out she was having me, she quit. Nursing school had taught her that everything you eat affects a baby, so she figured smoke probably would as well. We talked more over our cigarettes that afternoon than I ever remembered talking with my mother to that point and, when we finished, she said, "Now empty out this saucer and don't let me ever catch you smoking again."

Admittedly, I didn't immediately clean up my act after that encounter, but what stuck with me was her surprising approach to parenting through that situation and meeting me head-on by joining me at that table. She threw a curve ball at my intended rebellion and softened my edge, proving her adage that words are indeed consequential.

CHAPTER THIRTY-ONE
Float

W e were working on the homecoming float in the barn at Dillon's house at the top of our block where Bashford meets Old Farm Road. I'd promised my mother I'd never go back there after the incident in sixth grade when I was riding Sandy in the turn-out adjacent to the road and Dillon whipped the horse with a branch from the old oak tree that arched and twisted its canopy over much of the dilapidated farmhouse. Sandy took off galloping across the field, which is now an apartment complex called Legends, though I am quite sure few people know the legend of Sandy throwing me face-first into a pile of manure. Covered in green and brown shit laced with hay, I walked down Old Farm Road not meeting anyone's eyes with tears glistening in my own, knowing that Mom would say what she always said to me when a boy on our block was mean: "It's just that he likes you and he doesn't know how to show it."

But that isn't what she said this time. This time she said, "You are forbidden to go to Dillon's house ever again." But I had really wanted her to say the other thing, because I had a blossoming crush on Dillon and I hoped the reason for the horse whipping was his sign of reciprocal love.

Mom used the manure incident as the perfect opportunity to thwart such a romance. After all, Dillon's mom was a single woman and was known to have the occasional date or two. Mom didn't like the optics of Mrs. Kendrick standing on her rickety farmhouse porch in her tight jeans and tube top with her long hippie hair flowing to her waist, laughing with some man as they toasted *God knows what* with their bottles of Rolling Rock. I'm sure Mom thought they were toasting some unthinkable sex position, some clandestine maneuver that unmarried people did with the lights on while children were still within hearing distance, though they'd been sent out to play in the field alongside the sheep.

I didn't go back to Dillon's house for years after that, though I still tried to catch his eye across Mrs. Stone's class at Kingswood Sixth Grade Center or in the hallway at junior high as I came out of math and he emerged from science class. Once when I was miserably moping, Mom asked me if Dillon had ever apologized. The answer was no. But I told her yes, knowing that she'd surely tell me that any boy who would treat you that way wasn't worth your time. I guess I knew she was right, yet I still wasted a lot of my time trying to get his attention, taking the long way around the cafeteria past the table where I knew he'd be sitting with his friends on the football team en route to my seat next to the drama geeks.

Every time we drove to church, we'd pass by the farm and I'd look longingly at the crooked front porch, remembering the afternoons I'd spent drinking raspberry Kool-Aid on the rocking chairs or chasing chickens back into their coop. Occasionally I'd see Dillon or Mrs. Kendrick exercising the horses in the turn-out or galloping across the field and I'd long for that freedom. Or any freedom. It looked so much more like what my heart craved than heading to the confines of a hard wooden church pew.

But when we were in tenth grade and Mrs. Kendrick offered up her barn for the homecoming float building and I was a class officer, I kind of had to go. Surely four years later, the "never ever again" rule must have faded away. Surely there was enough water under the bridge between Dillon and me that we could move on from the manure. Surely Mom was too busy with my baby sisters to really notice. I decided what she didn't know wouldn't hurt her and, though I didn't lie when I said I was going to work on the float after dinner, I didn't tell her where said float-building was taking place.

The boys who were aces in woodshop demonstrated their construction skills by making the frame and wrapping our giant soon-to-be *jaguar riding in a paper maché model-T* in chicken wire while my friends and I cut squares of orange, black and white tissue paper to fill the holes with color.

The decorating was coming down to the wire. Homecoming was tomorrow and we were not done. It turned out, covering a 12-foot jaguar took a lot more paper squares than we thought and we'd have to work through the night. I lived the closest. All my other friends had to drive from their palatial homes with full basements in the north side of Raleigh. Dillon and I lived on the west side, amidst the tobacco and cotton fields where split-level and ranch homes that sold for $17,000 in the late 1960s and early 1970s were built amidst the pine trees on streets named after farm parts. I could walk home in less than five minutes and sneak in the back door as long as it wasn't too far past my 11 p.m. curfew. But time got away from me. Someone brought back pizza and I never checked my Swatch watch. Mrs. Kendrick came out with a case of beer and we took a break on the hay-bales for a bit. Again, I forgot to check the time. We were putting the final touches on the jaguar's ears when I finally did look at the time and it was 3 a.m. Oh crap! I ran home under cover of darkness, past Rail Fence Road to Hayloft Circle to find that the front porch light was off and all the doors were locked.

Was this a punishment? Sheesh. *I am in a shit-pile of trouble. I'm probably going to be grounded for a month! I'll miss the homecoming parade! I won't be able to go to the game or the dance! Mom will take my dress back to Hudson Belk! I'm going to get stuck doing the dishes for months.*

Or, maybe they didn't realize I was gone. If that were so, I surely shouldn't wake them up. I might be able to get away with this. I curled up on the deacon's bench on the front porch and used my brother's baseball glove as a pillow. I awoke abruptly as I heard my father opening the door for work. It was 5 a.m. and still dark. I dodged behind the forsythia bush before he made it out to the porch. After I saw his Bell South truck round the corner, I snuck back into the house and tiptoed up the stairs to my room, skipping the squeaky second-to-the-top step. My bedroom door was still closed. Perhaps they'd thought I was in there all along. There were no nasty notes left by my mother on my pillow. No signs anyone had even checked on me. My book bag was where I left it. Geez, apparently no one even tried to say goodnight to me. That's weird.

Ahh, but my journal appeared untouched under my mattress and the entries featuring my dreams of Dillon remained private as did my hope that I'd one day be more like Mrs. Kendrick, with her adventurous abandon, than like my mother with her chains to the church and to appropriate behavior.

CHAPTER THIRTY-TWO
Vow

W e're in the multipurpose room at Camp Seagull in Atlantic Beach, the smell of beans and franks still lingering in the air even after the chafing dishes have been cleared and the tables have been pushed along the wall to make room for the thirty or so of us tenth graders to sit cross-legged in a circle on the cool concrete floor.

"Now," says Father Bill. "We're going to go around the circle and sign our vows to stay chaste until marriage."

Father Bill is rather rotund with a huge bulbous nose that shines with oil. His glasses keep slipping down the glistening slope and he pushes them up with his Pillsbury Doughboy fingers every few seconds.

"He probably could never get a woman interested in him," Shane Walsh whispers in my ear. "That's why he married God."

I laugh nervously. Shane is super cute. I can't believe he just spoke to me. My heart is beating in my chest. I feel like I might pass out.

The clipboard is going around the room as Father Bill reads a passage from the Bible. Something about something thou shalt not do, but all I can think about is Shane's pink lips and the slight scent of cigarettes on his breath.

Shane is a bad boy. I'm not supposed to associate with bad boys.

The clipboard comes to him. He quickly and confidently scribbles his commitment and passes it on to me. *Hmmm.* I am surprised that someone like him is buying into all of this.

I look at his signature.

Eric Estrada, he wrote.

Farrah Fawcett, I write.

Later that night we make out in a sand dune.

CHAPTER THIRTY-THREE

Complexity

I did not commence my consumption of wine with a sophisticated palate. My first foray with the fruit of the vine was at the ripe age of fifteen and it was with a bottle of 1981 Boone's Farm Strawberry Hill. Actually, it could really be called a foray with the forbidden fruit because the beverage is an "apple wine product" that likely has *no* grapes in it.

It was a hot Saturday in late September, an Indian summer day when the leaves were yellowing but you could still catch whiffs of Hawaiian Tropic tanning oil emanating from the shiny brown legs of the teenagers smoking by the dumpster behind the 7-Eleven. Up until that fall, my only weekend outings were to slumber parties with girlfriends or to Skate Town, where we would roller skate in a cluster of neon to Chic's "Le Freak" and Queen's "Another One Bites the Dust," hoping to catch the eyes of the bad boys in baseball shirts and terry cloth headbands.

Once I got to high school, many of my parents' rules were mysteriously lifted. Once a straight-A student with a straightlaced reputation, I was suddenly unleashed upon the party scene and the only edicts I had to follow were to arrive home by curfew and to save myself for marriage. The possibility of alcohol consumption posing a challenge to rule number two was never discussed, though it would be many years and many, many more beers before I put serious thought into breaking that commandment.

But I embarked upon my newfound freedom with gusto. I hung out by the keg at my first high school parties, roach clip in my feathered hair, streaked orangey-yellow with Sun In, and my skin also an orangey-yellow from sunbathing on tinfoil with my body coated in baby oil and iodine.

I was determined to make my high school years memorable. I leaned in on the beer bongs when challenged, but I never actually liked beer, at least not the cheap stuff at high school parties. I drank it because it was present and plentiful, but I needed a beverage I could call my own.

So on that sticky hot September day when chrysanthemums dotted the flowerbeds and the last summer scents of honeysuckle were fading, a car full of junior and senior boys pulled up to the 7-Eleven, hanging out the windows and calling out to us, "Anyone up for a swim at Sugar Lake?"

"Sure!" we sophomores giggled back. We'd been in high school for less than a month and we'd already gotten the attention of the upperclassmen. This boded well for our social lives.

Within an hour, and without the use of cell phones to organize it, a caravan of ten cars and pickup trucks — their flatbeds filled with teens, towels, tubes and a pony keg — headed out to the old rock quarry otherwise known as Sugar Lake. Jody drove an old '62 white Porsche.

"Don't put your feet on the carpet," he called out as I climbed in, and we screeched down Buck Jones Road with Ozzy Osborne screaming about going off the rails on a crazy train.

When we were stopped at a traffic light, Jody lifted up the mat, revealing what was left of the corroded floorboard, a rusty web of metal that offered a good view of the asphalt one foot below. I tucked my feet up on the cracked leather seat as we turned onto the gravel road leading to the quarry and rocks hit the floormat like popcorn at first, then like machine gun bullets when Jody decided to race a red pickup truck with an empty gun rack across the back window.

A guy I didn't recognize was standing in the bed of the truck holding onto the gun rack with one hand while his other arm flew through the air, bucking-bronco style. The truck lurched as it sped in front of us, its coolers crashing against the right side of the bed as an inner tube bounced out into a horseweed-filled ditch. The flatbed cowboy was thrown to the metal floor as Jody and I stopped short in a cloud of dust to rescue the tube. The truck's driver hadn't noticed the loss of his cargo or potential injury to his passenger who, within moments, popped up with a *Yee-haw!* and cracked open one of the cans of Pabst Blue Ribbon that were floating in the pool of spilled ice.

We ducked one by one under the bent gap in the metal fencing, ignoring the *Do Not Enter* signs, and positioned our beach blankets and tattered towels on the lichen-covered rocks jutting out from the quarry cliffs and on the small stretch of beach below. Cases of beer and wine coolers were stationed on the large, flat rocks and someone passed me a bottle of icy cold Strawberry Hill. The sweet taste was far better than the bitterness of the beer, and I quickly became quite the connoisseur, easily identifying the nuanced notes that differentiated Tickle Pink from Sun Peak Peach while we drank out of Solo cups by the reservoir that was our teenage wasteland.

No one checked the water's depth before jumping. I guess we just believed the kid who said, "Trust me, I've been here before!" as he swan-dove off the highest ledge, followed immediately by several other credulous souls. I jumped in off a much lower precipice, holding my cup of wine-beverage high, and dog-paddled out to the nearest flotation device, keeping my fabulously feathered hair as dry as possible. There in a black rubber tube, with the Carolina-blue sky bright above me and the buzz of alcohol—along with the feeling of fitting in—settling into my lanky limbs, I felt contented and hopeful that high school wouldn't be as bad as I feared. Tiny fish nibbled at my butt, possibly foreshadowing some of the stings I'd suffer in the three years to come, but mostly I recall the easy sense of joy. A time when no choice seemed like a life changer. A time when we thought we were invincible.

As my new friends continued to leap off cliffs into the murky water, somehow avoiding the rocky edges, we all munched on Doritos and picante sauce and consumed boxes of Twinkies while listening to Steve Miller and Grateful Dead bootleg tapes on the boom box, smoking joints and Marlboro Lights. I captured memories with my Disc camera for my scrapbooks, the reckless wonder of our fleeting youth, developed weeks later and frozen in time.

We didn't know then that classmates would later die in drunk-driving accidents and others would lose their lives to cancer or fall victim to the soon-to-be known AIDS epidemic. Life was simple then. And so were our tastes.

And I wonder, as we grow older and take fewer risks—making smart adult decisions and slowly sipping Cabernet blends that come highly recommended by the sommelier at the local wine shop from lead-free crystal stemware meant specifically for the varietal you're drinking—is a more complex palate really all that much better if it comes with a more complex life? Maybe what we all need right now is to float in an inner tube with a Solo cup full of Tickle Pink and then follow the Cheerio trail back home.

CHAPTER THIRTY-FOUR
Twelve Steps

I saw my first penis when I was fifteen years old. I was behind the dumpster at Little Sue's Mini Mart, adjacent to the woods where the Goths from school would hang out smoking pot in their black trench coats with their black nail polish. My best friend Susan and I used to sneak cigarettes between that dumpster and the clump of trees, dipping ever so slightly into the dark side, but not enough for Susan to get kicked off the cheerleading squad. The afternoon of the "penis sighting," Susan had tucked a *Playgirl* under her chenille sweater as I bought us a pack of Salem Menthols to distract the cashier. When we got to our secluded dumpster hideaway, we flipped through the pages, at once surprised, repulsed and awed.

Ok, so maybe my first penis was just on glossy paper, but it left a lasting impression on me, though it had more immediate relevance for Susan. She had been spending time with our twenty-three-year-old science teacher after soccer practices. They'd made out a couple of times and there was some heavy petting. She wanted to know what it was she was touching through his jeans and, should she decide to take it further, she wanted to make sure she didn't betray her innocence with a shocked expression. Naively unaware of the inappropriateness of this relationship, I was just plain curious, and a bit envious that our hot biology teacher/soccer coach had shown interest in my clearly more mature friend.

The following weekend we went to a party at our friend Stuart's house. The AC/DC and Cheech & Chong flocked posters glowed in the blacklight as an orange and blue neon sign declared *It's Miller Time* over the well-stocked bar. There was a good chance that every vodka and gin bottle was no more than 20 percent liquor though, after months of teenagers slowly refilling what they'd consumed using water from the tap.

Susan and I were sitting on the couch puffing clove cigarettes and sipping our second or third lukewarm cup of Michelob Light and whispering about which of our classmates might have a penis worthy of being in a *Playgirl* centerfold. Susan went to get us each another beer from the keg. It was on its last legs in a big red bucket surrounded by a pool of water that once was ice, and she came back with a couple of cups that were mostly foam. We were debating who I might get to ask me to homecoming when the beer buzz sent Susan down an emotional rabbit hole and she began crying over the fact that she could never go anywhere public and certainly not to homecoming with the object of her affection. I stood up to get her a tissue, but as soon as I got to my feet, I fell back down. The room was spinning in a swirl of Bud and cloves.

What I don't recall is how I got home. What I do remember is that I totally missed my curfew. I also missed a step and fell into the grandfather clock in the entry hall, waking up the whole family, and then threw up on the black and white checkered linoleum floor.

Mom was furious. "My father was an alcoholic and I'm not going to allow the same fate for my child," she admonished as I sloppily and shamefully cleaned up the orange puddle of Budweiser and nacho cheese Doritos.

The next morning, I heard my mother on the phone with Susan's mom.

"These girls need to learn a lesson before they ruin their lives," Mom said.

Susan's mother must have agreed, because three days later, my mother dropped us off at what was supposed to be an Alcoholics Anonymous meeting on Hillsborough Street across from NC State University.

There we sat in a circle surrounded by a sad group of middle-aged women as the leader rose from her chair wearing a tweed blazer and called the meeting to order.

"We welcome you to the Raleigh Al-Anon family meeting and hope you will find in this fellowship help and friendship. We who live or have lived with the problem of alcoholism understand as perhaps few others can."

As they went around the room sharing painful stories about sloshed spouses, drunk dads, and sauced siblings, Susan and I looked at each other perplexed. This wasn't Alcoholics Anonymous. It was something else, and thankfully we had nothing remotely like their stories to share as we sat in our folding chairs wearing our high school sweatshirts amongst several women in rumpled t-shirts and sweatpants, some in business suits, and one tall redhead decked out in a cream-colored dress with Alexis Carrington shoulder pads. This was a tragic, heartbroken, miserable-but-supportive bunch, yet what were we supposed to say when they got to us? They were all one-upping each other with stories of flying plates and brandished weapons. We might have participated in a food fight with Planters Cheez Balls after over-indulging on some Boone's Farm Tickle Pink at the Lake Johnson dam, but no one got hurt. We didn't belong here.

At the first break, as the women crowded around the coffee dispenser and filled napkins with Chips Ahoy! cookies, we made a run for it, down a couple blocks and up a flight of stairs to Mitch's Tavern, where we tied our high school sweatshirts around our waists so we could easily pass for eighteen-year-old college girls and promptly ordered a pitcher of beer, laughing about the absurdity of our predicament. If only Susan's mother knew about our biology teacher. If only my mother knew about the stolen *Playgirl* hiding under my mattress and countless stolen looks at the penises within. They certainly wouldn't be so worried about us drinking beer, we laughed.

"Well, whatever I do, I will not marry a drunkard," I said.

"Whatever I do, I will not live in a trailer with a man who throws plates," said Susan.

We ducked into the campus mart for some squirty Freshen Up gum before meeting my mother at the designated pick-up spot.

"So, girls, how did it go?" she asked.

"Well, we learned a lot," we said. And that was the truth.

CHAPTER THIRTY-FIVE
On Giving My Maxx

I attempted multiple money-making schemes as a kid. I went door-to-door selling potholders and blanketed the neighbors' porches with hand-drawn flyers advertising my babysitting and dog-walking skills. My best friend and I even offered our services as piano teachers, though our expertise was limited to Books One through Five of the John W. Schaum *Making Music at the Piano* series and even our "Heart and Soul" duet lacked actual talent. Still, I thought I was qualified, having mastered basic versions of "Minuet in G" and "Für Elise." That scheme fizzled out when my one client, my neighbor Lynn (to whom I'd offered a free trial package) and I never got beyond our sloppy "Chopsticks" duet. It was clear that I could never approach her mother for renumeration.

But the month I turned fifteen, the most *amazing* thing happened. We were riding in Mom's Chevy Citation to pick up groceries from Winn-Dixie when it came on the radio: "*You get the max for the minimum, minimum price and it's never, ever the same place twice!*" Our town was getting a T.J. Maxx! Now I was going to have access to discounted designer brands. It was a game changer. But it gets better. When I got home from school a few days later, I found an ad torn from the newspaper on my strawberry quilt. T.J. Maxx was hiring and the minimum age to apply was fifteen! I set out to throw my soon-to-be marked-down hat in the ring.

The bright red backlit letters were just going up in front of the honey-colored stucco building as I navigated my way under the scaffolding and walked into an enormous space inhabited only by rows of partially assembled metal clothing racks and a folding table. Behind it, sitting on a folding chair, was a rather large black woman in a bold floral dress.

I took a deep breath. "I'm here to apply for a position with your company." I tried to sound confident. I tried to sound as if I'd had jobs other than babysitting and making potholders and lemonade.

She looked me up and down. Pastel pink dress, Sheer Energy nude pantyhose with reinforced toes, tan Candie's slip-ons that were indeed slipping on the recently polished gray vinyl floor, and a confirmation cross around my neck. She handed me an application and gestured toward another folding table near a partially built checkout counter. A guy in a red baseball cap, a wife-beater tank top, and jeans stained with grease sat in one chair. I felt overdressed as I sat down, picked up a pen, and leaned over to write my name. He looked up, craning his neck to see below the rim of his cap.

"You here to apply for a job?" he asked with a slow southern drawl.

"Yes." I smiled, not wanting to engage and needing to get my application submitted quickly. My mother and sisters were waiting in the car.

"I'm gonna try working the loading dock, settin' shit up, that kinda thang," he informed me. I suspected that might be a better job for him than customer service, but I didn't want to encourage a more in-depth conversation.

"Well, good luck," I said as I leaned into the application, feigning concentration.

Having no experience and only neighbors to list as references, it didn't take me long to finish. The man in the red cap was still working on his application when I slid my chair back under the table.

Two days after I turned fifteen, I returned for my interview. With my heart pounding and Mom again waiting in the Chevy, I walked under the now fully installed T.J. Maxx sign and into a space that resembled an actual store, with kiosks and wall racks, registers and hanging signage indicating where there would soon be dresses, menswear and coats.

The manager resembled a young Barney Fife, lanky and a little slouched, with a sad plaid tie hanging from his turtle-like neck. His hand was clammy when he shook mine and pointed to the rust-colored faux leather chair next to a stack of boxes that nearly touched the ceiling in his tiny office.

"So, what would you say you have to offer the T.J. Maxx team?" he asked with a serious expression.

"Well, I have a positive attitude and I am a team player," I explained, describing my role as sergeant-at-arms of my sophomore class, but leaving out my *Get High Vote Lowe* campaign slogan.

I was just about to share my love of fashion when there was a tap on the open door and the black woman who'd given me the application cleared her throat. "Your 3:35 is here."

I feared being rushed out without even having the chance to discuss my organizational skills when he said, "You're hired," and passed me an employment packet with a letter on top indicating my training day.

Two days later, I was set upon the boxes lining the aisles. For two weeks I worked diligently, eight hours a day, taking sweaters and slacks out of those boxes, putting them on hangers, and finding them homes on the racks between white circle size markers. I arranged socks by color and created visually appealing displays of handbags, hats and scarves.

As *Grand Opening* signs went up around town, I felt a real sense of pride in my work. When the store opened, I was there daily, as pretty much everyone in town came to check out Cary's newest retailer. I greeted guests with a smile, rehung dislodged dresses, and found mates for shoes scattered across the floor during the decision process.

But after the curiosity died down and the customer crush eased up, I noticed my fellow employees being called into Barney Fife's office, then walking out moments later, heads down, with sad or angry expressions. It turned out that they over-hired to stock and open the store, and they were in the process of firing excess employees. Three days went by and the parade seemed to be slowing down. I was gaining confidence, certain that management had observed my color coordination and gift for untangling fake gold necklaces.

Then on day four, my number was up. I was hooking the bands on a pile of rejected bras when the assistant manager tapped me on my shoulder. "You're wanted in the office." And so, with little eye contact and not even an offer to sit down, I was handed my check and told my services were no longer needed.

I'd never been fired before. I was a good student. I worked hard. Still, there I was, looking for a payphone to call home under the *Grand Opening* sign.

When I got into the car, Mom was quiet. "It's not your fault," she said kindly. "I'm sure you'll find another job."

T.J. Maxx was an early experience with failure, a lesson at a tender age that it is important to recognize when you are valued and when you're wasting your time. A lesson that sometimes you give your max and only get back the minimum.

CHAPTER THIRTY-SIX
No Flo

I am lying on the top of my sheets, fanning myself with V.C. Andrews' *Flowers in the Attic* and thinking that I can't imagine ever finding my brother attractive in that way. Gross. The symphony of crickets and frogs outside my window is the only break from the thick summer stillness. There is rarely a breeze in the heavy August air on our cul-de-sac. Heat rises, they say, and in our split-level house, it comes up like an elevator from hell, climbing the narrow staircase and stagnating in my room. Across the hall, my parents' air-conditioned bedroom lures me with the magical coolness that blows onto my incessantly sticky legs when I steal a nap on their queen-sized bed under the giant cross of Jesus with the bloody feet. The cool blasts of air send me on a drowsy journey to the North Pole as goosebumps rise on my forearms like braille and I feel like Eloise at The Plaza.

In those summer days of old, we kids headed out in the morning, roaming wild about the 'hood, exploring the cement tunnels that were abandoned sewer pipes where we'd catch crawdads as we straddled the mere half foot of murky water. Kids crisscrossed the sidewalks on bicycles, Big Wheels, and strap-on metal roller skates. Dad took the wheels off a pair my brother and I had cranked to their farthest setting and clearly outgrown and screwed the wheels onto a narrow piece of plywood and called it a skateboard. Billy bumped down the cul-de-sac and crashed into the Evil Knievel ramp that the Kenney boys had made out of two-by-fours left over from their equally haphazardly designed tree house.

At dusk, dinner bells rang on back stoops across Old Farm and moms would call out "Suzie! Billy! Time for dinner!" or "Kenney boys, get your butts home *now*!" Mr. Anderson shouted down the street, his booming ex-Marine voice echoing off the lampposts just flickering to life, and home we'd all run or ride or skate or skulk, depending what you were going home to. Perhaps it was a tuna casserole served with silence, perhaps it was lukewarm SpaghettiOs from the can, or perhaps it was a belt-licking, as I later learned was often the case for the Andersons.

Many a summer day I'd sit under the shade of the pines on the hill beside my house, lazily scratching at mosquito bites and plotting my next get-rich-quick schemes. Mom said lemons were too expensive for our lemonade stand, but when Country Time launched their powdered drink mix in the late 1970s, our business took off and you could find members of my Girls' Club flagging down cars along Old Farm Road on lazy August afternoons. By the time I was twelve, I was a regular on the babysitting circuit when I wasn't doing the job for free for my mother.

Once I was in high school, I aspired to have my own air-conditioning unit in my own bedroom. The Sears catalog had one for sale for $300, which would take about one hundred and fifty hours of babysitting. I needed a better job now that T.J. Maxx had crushed my dreams.

When the *Help Wanted* sign went up at the Golden Corral shortly after I'd been fired, I saw my chance. I'd seen *Flo* and *It's A Living*. Waitressing seemed like it could be glamorous. But I didn't realize I'd have to work my way up to the job. At my interview, I was offered a job as the "soup or salad girl." My manager, Mr. San Filipo, told me that I was the first face customers would see and that I set the tone for their dining experience. As soon as they picked up their trays and utensils, I was to brightly smile and inquire, "Would you like a soup or salad with your meal?" Then I'd hand over a plate for the salad bar or a bowl for one of the two soups of the day, usually chicken noodle or broccoli cheese, which, at the start of my shift, I will have dumped out of a large metal can three times the size of the largest Chock full o' Nuts coffee tin and into the black kettle so that the congealed mass had time to soften before the lunch or dinner rush. At the end of the night, Sheldon, the bus boy, soaked the cheese and noodles that were crusted on the sides of the cauldrons until we filled them again the next day.

Once customers were armed with their melamine plates or bowls, if indeed they said yes—and I really hoped they did because Mr. San Felipo had told me that the more soups and salads I sold, the sooner I could move up to waitress—I'd then guide customers' gazes to a delicious array of dessert choices: cheesecake, German chocolate cake, or chocolate pudding with a dollop of whipped cream and a maraschino cherry on top. I was one of those filling the bowls, squirting the cream, placing the cherries, and cutting the cakes. The slices had to be precisely the right size. If we mis-cut, the slice could not be served and so, back behind the fridge, the line cooks and greeters like myself feasted on uneven pieces. I gained ten pounds in two months eating crooked carrot cake and blobs of German chocolate frosting. When I needed a salt fix, I'd pour chunky blue cheese dressing over croutons and eat the concoction with a spoon. Who needs to waste money on a 50 percent-off meal during our thirty minute break?

On those sweltering days of summer when I wasn't working and I could eke out minutes under the air conditioner in my parents' room with a book, I was in my bliss. But when I looked at the clock and saw that I only had fifteen minutes to get to work, the cool comfort evaporated for the sweaty panic of my bedroom, where I'd pop open a new L'eggs egg, because it wasn't ladylike to go anywhere in a dress without stockings. It is hard to pull stockings over sweat, but at least fresh L'eggs aren't steak-scented like my brown uniform.

If I ever want that waitressing gig, I can't be late. I rush to the front porch where my white nursing shoes sit, disallowed in the house after my mother found a trail of grease when our dog, Barkley Beau Lowe, followed me around the house after my first shift like I was a strange blend of she who feeds him *and* his food. That is not surprising. Work in a place like the Golden Corral and you will see ribeyes that fall on the floor and are picked up by the "chef" and thrown back on the grill. And those white nurse's shoes have to walk through the grease splatter to get to the carpeted floor where the waitresses smile jauntily like MTV VJs, collecting their tips and looking snidely at those of us who work behind the counter. They didn't get the view behind the scenes. They didn't know they were serving steaks off the floor.

At $3.10 an hour, working about twenty-five hours a week in the summer, I made what I needed to get that air conditioner, but realized that I'd really rather have Gitano jeans and some Esprit sweaters to complete my post-Labor Day Back-to-School look. I was so hungry for fashion as the weather cooled down and the networks debuted their new fall lineups with jingles like ABC's "Still The One" montage featuring Robin Williams, Danny DeVito, Hal Linden and Cheryl Ladd. I decided to reduce my hours so I could keep making spending money but still be in all the clubs I loved. I asked my manager if he'd consider me for a promotion to waitress, and he told me I needed at least three more months of experience passing out soup plates and salad bowls.

Three months later, he told me he was fully staffed but to ask again next month. The next month he told me business was down and we really needed to sell more soup and salads. If I could use my charm to up our numbers, he'd consider me the following month.

I left after a year, having never achieved my dream of becoming the next Flo.

CHAPTER THIRTY-SEVEN
America's Next Top Black + Decker Hand Model

The spring of my Junior year, I was chosen to represent my high school on the Teen Board of a local department store. It was a dream come true. We got to model the latest spring and fall fashions in runway shows and pose in prom dresses in the local newspaper. With my new role came the opportunity to work in the store. I was able to leave the greasy floors of my job peddling soups and salads at Golden Corral for the shiny marble sales floor of Ivey's.

I started out as a floater, selling cookie sheets and bed sheets in Housewares, lacy bras and coordinating panties in Lady's Lingerie, and pinstriped shirts in the Men's Department. I eventually landed my dream job in the Junior Department, where K-Tel music mixes played on an endless loop and I got to dress mannequins in Calvin Klein jeans, velour joggers and Members Only jackets.

It was there, as I was ringing up the sale of a leopard print dress with quarterback-worthy shoulder pads to a woman with a huge perm, that I was *discovered*. The woman called out to a man by the acid washed jeans, "Honey, come here and see her hands." I looked at them as I draped a hanging bag over the dress, my hot pink nails clicking against the hanger. They looked pretty normal to me.

"You have exceptionally lovely fingers," she said to me. The man, who was wearing his Ray Bans indoors, raised them to his forehead and reached his palms toward me.

"May I see?" he asked as I quizzically placed my hands in his. "Ah, yes indeed!" he commented, carefully examining my fingers and my wrists, adorned with a dozen neon-colored rubber bracelets. "Here's my card," he said, handing me the first business card I'd ever encountered. "Call me tomorrow, please. I'm a photographer and I'm looking for a model for a campaign I need to shoot this weekend."

Me! A model?! I'd always dreamed there might be a modeling agent in the audience at the fall Back-To-School fashion show, as Cyndi Lauper sang about girls having fun over the mall loudspeakers and shoppers in the food court watched with minimal interest as I twirled awkwardly in my parachute pants on the makeshift runway. Maybe I'd be discovered and find myself in *Seventeen* alongside my idols Kristy McNichol, Brooke Shields, and Mariel Hemingway. Sadly, no one seemed to think I was the next IT Girl except my mother and her best friends, who came to every show and waved eagerly as I tried to look professional and aloof like I imagined Elle Macpherson might on a Paris runway.

But then this happened and I had a business card to prove it. I couldn't contain myself. I was seventeen and I was about to hit the big time. I could feel it! As I drove home from work in my rusty red 1967 Mustang, my heart was pounding with excitement. I showed the card to my mother.

"It's a scam," she said. "I'm sorry honey, but men do this type of thing to lure pretty girls into precarious situations."

"But he was with his wife!" I protested.

We went back and forth until I finally convinced her to let me make the call. We agreed that I'd meet with them at the photo studio with my mother accompanying me.

The studio turned out to be legitimate. My hands were photographed for a Black + Decker campaign and I spent three days holding drills, sanders and other power tools. I was paid $250 each day, more than I made in two months working part time at Ivey's when minimum wage was $3.35 an hour. Several months later, I was called back to hold paint brushes for an art supply store shoot, and during winter break my freshman year in college, I modeled mood rings.

These gigs nearly paid for two years of college, but I was deeply disappointed. On the stages adjacent to mine, beautiful women were flashing smiles for the camera, cocking their heads just so, looking coy and cute, wearing stylish clothes and making them look perfect. They were wanted for more than just their hands, but no matter how I dressed or smiled, I was never elevated beyond hand model and my career ended abruptly after I broke one of my precious (and uninsured) fingers playing a game of flag football in front of Morrison dorm in the spring of freshman year. We set my pinky with a Popsicle stick and scotch tape and went on with the game, and I never got another chance to make power tools look sexy.

CHAPTER THIRTY-EIGHT

Silverfish

Aunt Joanne gave us the silverfish. She came down from Manhattan with a suitcase full of stylish dresses and expensive outfits from Lord & Taylor for my brother and me, along with a school of silverfish that must have climbed aboard the brown leather vessel from the recesses of her cedar-lined Upper East Side apartment closet. They marched out onto the hardwood floors of our two-story house on Hayloft Circle and straight into the linen closet. They paraded up the walls dotted with mom's macramé planters and her rough rendition of Van Gogh's "Sunflowers" that was created in her oil-painting class at the Raleigh Civitan Center while my brother and I were stuck in Vacation Bible School at the Baptist church even though we were Catholic. Free childcare came with the opportunity for salvation.

But after Aunt Joanne's visit, nothing could save us from the silverfish. They darted out of *National Geographics* and scurried onto couch cushions. The slithering shiny annoyances feasted on bookbindings, carpet, photographs and dandruff. They multiplied like freckles after a summer in the sun, and for years, every time Mom would crush one under her Sunday bulletin, she'd mutter her annoyance at her sister who'd left the gift that kept on giving.

To me, Aunt Joanne was just another adult who showed up on holidays and asked me what my favorite class was in school, then took off on some tangent about her own education that didn't interest me. Aunt Joanne's stories were peppered with the names of famous people who'd graced her path and the fabulous places she'd been. Her date with Dick Van Patten, who we loved on *Eight is Enough*. The meals she'd eaten in the Rainbow Room with its magical views and legendary chandeliers. But her stories were also tinged with bitterness.

When she was five, she contracted polio and was sent to a hospital where the Daughters of Wisdom swore she'd get more therapy than was available to a bricklayer's baby in Brooklyn. Surely my grandparents thought they were doing what was best for their child, explained my mother in defense of her parents.

But Aunt Joanne, fifteen years my mother's senior, remembers it differently. Mom didn't know how the nuns tortured Joanne, forcing her legs painfully straight and pushing her to exertion beyond her little child limits. After all, Mom's pictures of her sister's plight were painted by my grandmother, who was equally a victim, having had to send her baby away.

As a little girl, Joanne McGrath felt she'd been abandoned. And despite her Elizabeth Taylor looks as a teen and young woman, her limp stripped away those beauty advantages and colored her perception of life the hazy gray of a winter's sunset—though she clearly enjoyed sharing her elaborate stories of hobnobbing with the affluent and I often thought it amazing that she'd overcome her affliction to achieve such successes. My mother would wonder aloud after Aunt Joanne's visits were over, "Was she making all that up to impress us?"

She was animated when talking about dinner at Lutèce and tea at the Waldorf, but when it came to talking about family, she forever found ways to poke thorns into happy memories and add boulders atop the soil of sadness. She patently resented the easier life of her younger sister, polio free, with parents doting solely on her once her older siblings had left to make lives for themselves in other New York City boroughs.

Joanne severed ties with my mother after their parents died. I'd heard she'd moved to California, and a decade later, when I too landed on the West Coast, I decided to look her up. Surely no relationship is beyond salvage. Young and optimistic, I was.

I found her in Pasadena, relatively close to my apartment in Hollywood. She walked with a cane and told me in no uncertain terms that mentioning my mother was off limits. But what else connected us? Sitting in the Rusty Pelican adjacent to the 134 Freeway, I bristled at the admonition but was determined to make some kind of connection. After all, she was my godmother, though she now professed to be an atheist.

I encouraged her to share stories of relatives I'd never met and the family history I only had vague knowledge of. I learned that Great-Grandpa Flynn's home was sold to pay back taxes to a horrible woman named Tootsie Zorilla, who covered the once stately house in asbestos shingles and enclosed the wraparound front porch, my Great-Grandma Flynn's pride and joy, with bricks and stucco.

Joanne's stories brought to life the family skeletons nestled in the closet along with the silverfish. She said their cousin Regina once told my great-grandmother that she'd been raped following a Broadway audition and was then committed to a State Hospital for the mentally insane, where she eventually died.

Some of what Aunt Joanne shared was fascinating. Other stories sounded outlandish or were mean-spirited and likely meant to alter my perception of some of the relatives I know my mother had loved.

According to Joanne, Cousin Bobby's contractor business had to have been backed by the Mafia because he didn't have the smarts to set it all up on his own, having inherited my

Great-Grandfather McGrath's low level of intelligence. Mom had worshipped her grandpa.

Uncle Arthur had webbed fingers, which was likely a sign of mixed blood or inbreeding, which Aunt Joanne thought more likely of my father's Tennessee relatives than her side of the family, "but of course there are exceptions to every rule."

Many years later, well after my mother died and a Christmas card to my aunt was returned to sender several months after the holidays and a call to her apartment revealed a disconnected line, I used Google Earth to find the name of her retirement complex and called the main office. It turns out Aunt Joanne carried her bitterness and loneliness with her to the grave. She had died several months earlier, leaving instructions not to contact her next of kin and to give all of her belongings to charity. I looked at our last correspondence, just days before her body was found, and I was grateful I'd asked so many questions about our family history even though I'm not sure what parts of her responses were true and what stories were fabrications. Little shimmering, shiny annoyances left lingering in my memory like silverfish.

CHAPTER THIRTY-NINE
Freedom to Ride

It happened at least half a dozen times every winter. The weather forecasters would predict snow and I'd hedge my bets and not do my homework. Instead, I'd relax watching *The Apple Dumpling Gang* or *Escape from Witch Mountain* on *The Wonderful World of Disney* then stare out my bedroom window and pray that heavy, starless skies would produce a winter wonderland by morning.

Sometimes we'd get lucky and wake up late, squealing with delight at a ground blanketed in white. If it was deep enough, we knew that homework could wait a few more days, and we'd layer tights under Toughskins and turtlenecks under sweaters and sled down the cul-de-sac with one kid stationed at the bottom to shout "Car!" before anyone got crushed. We'd make snow angels and lumpy snowmen until our toboggans were topped with icicles and our cheeks and fingertips were pink with frostbite. We'd head into the house and drink hot chocolate while our clothes dried. Nothing felt better than heading out to sled with a warm belly and clothes straight out of the dryer.

When Mom didn't trust the weather forecast and hadn't stocked up for the storm, we'd trudge up Buck Jones Road—long before I-40 rerouted the road into an overpass—to Winn Dixie for milk and whipped cream, that is unless we were willing to accept her powdered milk.

More often than not, though, that first glance out the window was a crushing disappointment and I'd have to scramble to make my homework appear at least attempted, or I'd have to fake illness, burying my head under pillows and blankets until I was credibly sweaty and feverish. But snow wasn't the only way out. If sleet turned to ice as the temperature dipped, we might still be in luck. Shiny asphalt on Old Farm Road offered hope, because in Wake County in the 1970s and 1980s, school buses were driven by high school students. Thirty unbelted little bodies were in the care of eighteen-year-olds who were happy to get out of first and seventh periods to earn extra cash. Their maximum of two years of driving experience was a jackpot for a kid needing a snow day, because ice anywhere in the county could result in countywide school closures.

The bus drivers at my high school got their initial education in the school's driver's education classes under the instruction of Mr. Piver, the physical education teacher who wore his striped athletic socks to his knees and his white-piped satin gym shorts too high on his thighs while showing us gruesome films with names like "Red Asphalt" and "Carnage on the Freeway" of the aftermath of car accidents, with those final images of a prom corsage lying on the pavement in a pool of blood. He then loaded us, four at a time, into the school's tan Datsun equipped with an extra brake pedal on the passenger's side. With three classmates in the back of the car and Mr. Piver yelling at them to "Calm down! You'll get your turn!" it was difficult to concentrate. Archelus McClean ran over a mailbox on his first attempt at parallel parking. My palms were sweating when I took the wheel, knowing that I had three young witnesses to any unsteady move, and any serious or comical mistake would haunt me in the cafeteria and hallways for weeks to come.

While many kids had been driving on family farms or country roads since they were nine or ten, driver's ed was my first time behind the wheel. When I had my permit, my father finally took me to the mall parking lot, which was generally empty on Sundays because of the state's Blue Laws. I promptly headed for the one car parked under a tree before veering off my path and nearly giving him a heart attack. I was not a confident driver, yet rumor had it that the DMV would give a license to a goat, so it was with only a little apprehension that I set out to get my driver's license right after school on my sixteenth birthday.

Everything went smoothly at first. I aced the written test while Mom waited in the Chevy Citation. Then Mom got out and the DMV lady got in and off we went, out of the parking lot and down Blue Ridge Road. The examiner was no-nonsense. She didn't abide by my friendly chatter or nervous laughter. So I quietly clicked my blinker, making left and right-hand turns. I parallel parked without hitting anything, including the curb.

But ten minutes into my driving test, things took a turn when my mother's stupid car conked out. I suspect the lady in the shotgun seat was wishing she'd worn different shoes, though surely she only anticipated walking from her counter to the car and back again about twenty times that day. There I was with my driving examiner carrying her clipboard, small beads of sweat forming on her upper brow and threatening to cascade down her cheek past her bright pink lips in a salty waterfall as we walked across the overpass. Her thick ankles were swollen in the heat as she trudged past the barbed wire-topped fences of the Youth Detention Center in her navy-blue pumps. She couldn't have known that the vehicle she was riding in with me would sputter and die three quarters of a mile from the DMV office, and just an hour and a half before she could call it quits for the long Memorial Day weekend. How unfortunate that when the number fifty-seven came up, she was the next examiner.

I was walking next to her, trying to hold back the tears. Ten minutes earlier, my hair and makeup were just perfect for the photo that I planned to proudly display for all of my friends and family at my party that evening. I could taste my freedom. Freedom to ride! I was wearing the new birthday top and skirt my mother had bought me the day before at the Town Center Mall, where I'd perfected my driving skills. "I still say that skirt is too short," Mom muttered as she handed the clerk at The County Seat $21.95 in exact change. I had a bright blue ribbon tied around my side braid to match the stripes on my shirt.

But we had gone less than a mile when the car began shaking. My palms were sweating as the instructor asked me to pull over by the side of the road. We barely cleared the asphalt before the car simply stopped. I turned the key in the ignition. Nothing. The instructor got out of the car and I opened my door as a Pine State milk truck whizzed by, dust and leaves swirling in the muggy air.

"Let me try," she grumbled as I stood along the gravel-strewn shoulder, kicking at a Burger King French fry cup.

"This can't be happening," I kept saying to myself. But it was. My sixteenth birthday was ruined.

The examiner looked at me with contempt as she handed me the keys to my parents' piece of crap car and we began the trek back to the DMV offices, passing the livestock pavilion at the state fairgrounds on the left and then the Waffle House just beyond the bend on the right.

Cars in working condition passed at alarming speeds as we plodded along the shoulder. Drivers with licenses confidently tucked in their wallets came flying by within inches of my purse with no license.

The examiner was seething, muttering under her breath and panting profusely, her rather large bottom swaying in front of me in her blue, beige and tan zigzag-print skirt as we crossed the overpass in a single file march to my doom. As we approached the DMV, I saw my mother sitting on the concrete bench in front of the cement block building, thumbing through her *Better Homes and Gardens* magazine. She looked at me quizzically as we trudged down the sidewalk. The examiner wiped her brow with the back of her hand, shaking her head at my mother, and I heard her say something about automobile maintenance and irresponsibility and wasting her time.

My mother looked at me with a mixture of pity and relief as she pulled a dime out of her change purse for the pay phone. "Well, she wasn't very pleasant," Mom said as she dialed my father's office. "You can try again in a few months, honey."

A few months?! I was devastated to be so close to the precipice of independence and to have it yanked away because of a crappy car.

When I finally got my license, the first thing I did was drive to the Mini Mart down the street from our house to pick up a four-pack of wine coolers before driving to my best friend's house to celebrate. The drinking age was eighteen but no one ever checked IDs and at sixteen in heels, I didn't need a fake one. Ah, but I finally had a license and I could taste the delicious promise of freedom.

CHAPTER FORTY
Fat Looks Better When It's Tan

My mother is sitting in her yellow mesh metal-framed lawn chair, the rotating spray from the sprinkler catching her toes every three to four minutes. Her thighs are as pink as uncooked hotdogs. Specks of sunlight shine through her straw beach hat and onto her chest where they dance with her freckles. My baby sister is asleep in her playpen under the canopy of the crab apple and cherry trees.

Our neighbor Joy walks across the street with a mason jar filled with freshly made Lipton Sun Tea. "You're plenty pink there, Dottie," says Joy.

"Oh, it'll turn tan," responds my mom. "And you know what I always say, 'Fat looks better when it's tan!'" They laugh.

I look at my thighs. At twelve, they haven't got much shape. Beanpoles, my dad calls my legs. My towel is soaked as ripples of sprinkler water wash over me from head to toe on the return trips from Mom's side of the yard. My ankles and calves are covered with short green specks of freshly cut grass.

Mom hasn't lost the baby weight in the nearly two years since my sister was born. She's taken to wearing bathing suits with skirts. Wheat germ, brown rice and carob chips replace the Velveeta and Chips Ahoy! that were staples of my early childhood diet.

Prevention magazines fill the bathroom rack. My dad grumbles about the good old days when Sloppy Joes on Wonder Bread buns were a typical dinner. The next night Mom makes "Soy Joes" that are mostly mushrooms and tomato sauce served on whole wheat buns. It doesn't go over well. We're all famished.

"Children are starving in Africa," Mom reminds us. She pins a photo of an emaciated child with a swollen belly to the fridge as a reminder, but we are pretty certain that little boy wouldn't enjoy Mom's cabbage-stuffed green peppers either.

I find my mother's stash of peanut butter cups under the sink and eat them all. She knows I know but she doesn't say anything, embarrassed, I'm sure, that her little secret has been discovered. Later I find a new stash in the Crock-Pot atop the hutch. Again, she says nothing when they slowly but surely disappear.

A year later I am in ballet class. The mirror is there to ensure our posture is good and our toes are pointed, but I'm not looking at myself. I can't keep my eyes off Carol Connor. My long, skinny legs give way to pudge around my belly, cut in half by the elastic of my tights. My brother and I have rebelled against the spelt bread and almond butter sandwiches that Mom puts in our lunch boxes. No one wants to trade their Cheez Puffs or egg salad with us, so we spend our allowance on Snickers and Zero bars at Little Sue's Mini Mart.

Unlike me, Carol has breasts, a flat stomach and hips. I can't keep my eyes off of her. I wonder if this magical thing called puberty that Judy Blume keeps promising is heading my way anytime soon. I hope it will make me look like Carol. But after a year of dancing side-by-side with her—Carol gliding with perfect jetés, her breasts gently bouncing on the landings, and me jumping and landing with a thud—I still don't need a bra.

Mom makes her own yogurt, covers dinner salads with bean sprouts and serves them with bran muffins. One month, butter is bad for us and the next month she subtracts the yolks from our scrambled eggs. We sneak to the neighbors' for Doritos and Ho Hos. I look forward to my babysitting jobs at the Suttons because Mrs. Sutton always leaves TV dinners to microwave. Mom says the radiation from those frozen meals will kill me if the Salisbury steak doesn't get me first.

Eventually, Mom gives into the grumbling in the house and starts buying the things we like to eat. The Grape-Nuts go stale in the back of the pantry and we're devouring Froot Loops. I am back to eating real PB&J or my favorite lunch of liverwurst and mayonnaise on white bread with a Hostess blueberry pie for dessert.

When I am seventeen, I am chosen to represent my high school on the local department store's Teen Board. At the first meet and greet they take our measurements. We'll be modeling the latest fall fashions in a runway show. As a *Seventeen* magazine devotee, I am excited. I'd been a regular in the dressing rooms of the Junior Department and I think of myself as pretty average in my size nine corduroys. But as the measurements of my fellow models are taken, the costumer calls out, "Julie is a size 3; Megan is a size 3; Anna will need a size 5; Leilani's a size 1; and Suzanne will need a 9."

I realize just how much bigger I am compared to my peers. Mom and I always laughed at the tiny sizes on the racks. "Why would they make Guess jeans to fit 5-year-olds?" we joked. I didn't realize that actual people fit into them.

There weren't plus-size models back then, but it seems obvious to me that I have been selected to demonstrate size diversity. I am only two sizes away from the largest size they carry in the Junior department, a 13. I start watching what I eat. Mom seems happy that I appear to be jumping aboard the carrot and celery train.

Until carrots and celery are practically all that I eat. And people begin to notice. "You look good! Have you lost weight?" "Oh my gosh, you're so skinny!" It feels good. My clothes loosen. I go down a size. Then they stop noticing.

Obviously, I need to lose more weight to hold their interest. But to do that, I need to eat less. Signing up for even more after-school activities allows me to skip dinner. "We're grabbing a pizza," I tell my mother, or "I'm eating at Chrissie's."

If I eat anything, I need to work it off. I have a cookie and chase it down with a hundred sit-ups. I have a slice of pizza at an afterschool rehearsal and I run three miles. But with school and clubs and practices and rehearsals and my job, I'm running out of time to run.

Vomiting is far more efficient. And you can actually eat more. Two slices of pizza, stick your fingers down your throat and get back to work, guilt free.

I pick out a prom dress, white and strapless. Lace and chiffon. Size 5. I feel beautiful.

I am in a non-stop whirl with senior activities, Teen Board fashion shoots, and waiting to hear from the three colleges I applied to. I am fueled by my exquisite self-control and purpose.

In three months, I have lost thirty pounds. I begin to wear baggy sweatshirts to hide my bony hips. Mom is concerned. She takes me to my pediatrician who tells me that if I lose any more weight, we may have a problem. The next month I put rocks in my pockets and wear ankle weights under my MC Hammer pants. When I step on the scale, I pass inspection.

The week before prom, I try on my dress. It won't stay up. My breasts have shrunk to their prepubescent size. Mom takes me to get it altered. I see the look of concern on her face. We go to lunch at Ashworth Drugs. She knows their pimento cheese sandwich and chocolate shake are my favorites. At least they used to be. She watches me as I eat, taking tiny sips and nibbling around the edges, chewing more than I need to. I excuse myself as she waits for the check and puke up lunch in the bathroom.

Even with the alterations, we have to use a safety pin to keep my prom dress secure. My boyfriend takes me to the elegant Velvet Cloak Inn with its New Orleans-inspired wrought-iron railings and crystal chandeliers. It's a lovely, romantic dinner and surely the most expensive date we've ever been on. Before we head to the Marriott for the dance, I stick two Lee Press-On nail-covered fingers down my throat and regurgitate my three courses, careful not to splash the second iteration of Caesar salad, lobster sauce and chocolate cake on my frothy white dress.

That night I realize things have gone too far. My boyfriend, in all his earnestness, worked extra hours to pay for a meal I flushed down the toilet. The small sizes I can now fit into don't look good on my bony frame. My relationship with food is as tenuous as my relationship with my mother. Things that were supposed to stay down and never come up are beginning to surface.

Mom leaves newspaper clippings about the death of Karen Carpenter just a year earlier on my bed. After years of struggling with anorexia, Karen's heart just gave out. In photos of the iconic singer with the crystal-clear voice, it becomes clear to me that it is possible to be too thin. Beyond Twiggy-thin. Less-than-a-size-zero thin.

While this is about food, it is also about something deeper for me. It is about exercising control where I never felt I had it. It is reflective of more than the image I see in the mirror, a funhouse mirror where a too-fat girl looks back, even though the scale clearly says I'm not fat.

In the mid-1980s, there is little access to information about— or support for—anorexia and bulimia. Remarkably, I am one of the lucky ones. I exorcise my eating disorder demons when I leave home for college and develop a somewhat healthier relationship with food outside my mother's fluctuating parameters. I don't subscribe to fad diets, I try to consider the value of food as fuel, and I make an effort not to punish myself for enjoying the occasional or even regular treat.

However, once the seeds are planted, distorted self-image and a complicated connection to food sprouts up like an unwelcomed weed throughout a lifetime.

There's the guilt that accompanies an unpurged binge. There's the guilt when a purge isn't prevented. There's the ordering of salads on dates when you really want the pasta. There's the time when you order pasta and fervently wish you hadn't. There's the wedding dress you still wish fit differently a decade hence and then the baby weight that may or may not come off. There's the turning every window into a mirror and never being happy with what you see. And there's the dressing room and the stack of bathing suits. Turning this way and that, trying to hold your stomach in with an eyeroll and a resigned grimace. There's the decision that you refuse to resort to a suit with a skirt, but that a tan might help. In that case, perhaps, mother knew best.

CHAPTER FORTY-ONE
Mistaken Identity

My freshmen roommates, Catherine and Stacy, and I are in the final stage of unpacking and climbing up and down the ladders to the loft that Stacy's father built to make it possible for us to fit three eighteen-year-old girls in one 10x10 room with space for a couch between the desks below. As I was lining up my cassette tapes in a gap between 2x4s of the loft frame, there was a knock at the door. A pretty girl with long black hair stood there.

"Is Suzanne home?" she asked.

"That's me." I smiled.

She paused and eyed me oddly. "Uh, ok, well uh, we'd like to invite you to this mixer next Friday," she said as she handed me a flyer, her quizzical look still awkwardly apparent.

It wasn't until I'd said goodbye and closed the door that I realized why she reacted that way. My hair was corn-silk yellow. The mixer I'd been invited to was for the Carolina American Indian Club. I didn't fit the image. I rolled my eyes and thought back to my mother's scheme in the spring of 1979. I balled up the paper and threw it in the trash.

Sure I was one eighth Cherokee, but that was just one part of my heritage, woven through the nuggets of family lore that were revealed piecemeal in rare conversations with distant relatives over sweet tea on the Astroturf-covered carport at Grandma's house in Tennessee. "Tell me about our family history?" I'd ask. The stories were vague. No one seemed to know a lot.

The vagaries of our understanding of my Dad's heritage were not surprising. What we knew was that his biological father was half Cherokee, but Dad's mother died of breast cancer when she was thirty-five and my father was only eight. His father, who'd outlived two previous wives, was seventy-nine at the time of his third wife's death. The county placed his four children up for adoption and into foster care. Their names were changed, and they didn't grow up together. Records of our Cherokee blood were said to have burned in a fire on the reservation. But I grew up knowing that *my* people were Appalachian Indians, the part of the tribe that successfully hid in the hills to avoid the Trail of Tears. It was a point of pride to come from such strong and stealthy stock.

When we played Cowboys and Indians as children, my brother and I dodged the cap gun "bullets" from the neighborhood kids on bicycle horses as we shot arrows from the bows we'd gotten on our summer trip to the Oconaluftee Village in Cherokee, North Carolina. Like our Native American father, we proudly rooted for the Washington Redskins and the Atlanta Braves.

Back in time, in 1965, my Irish Catholic, Brooklyn-born mother was ostracized for marrying outside her race. In my dad Bill's hometown, the racial thing wasn't so much the issue. My aunt recalls a group of women approaching her shortly after the wedding.

"Oh Ann, we're so sorry to hear about Billy!"

"What do you mean?" she asked.

"Oh, heavens child, we hear he went and married him a *Catholic!*"

Well, that Catholic and that Baptist went and had them some kids and the Irish DNA clearly won out.

Now in 1979, when I was heading into seventh grade, our lower-middle class, mostly white neighborhood was slated to be bused into downtown Raleigh. Most of my friends from elementary school were going to the junior high just five minutes from our home. My mother was livid. Why did they arbitrarily choose our neighborhood for the forty-five-minute bus ride? Did they think there wouldn't be a fight because we were working class? She wrote letters. She spoke to the school board. "How can we be expected to be part of our kids' education when it'll take more than an hour to get to and from a PTA meeting?" she asked. Her reasoning was rejected. The school district was obligated to integrate and this was how they'd decided to do it.

Then Mom cooked up a scheme. "Well," she decided, "if what they want are minorities, I've got your minorities."

In many states, at least back then, a child's race was automatically entered on the birth certificate as the mother's. Mom filed paperwork to change my brother's and my race to American Indian. After all, she explained, Willie Nelson was recently named "American Indian of the Year" and his blood flowed with as much Cherokee as ours. I'd long been proud to have blood coursing through my veins that connected me with the stealthy natives who hid in the hills rather than endure the deadly Trail of Tears. Maybe I, too, was a resilient and resourceful warrior?

Mom petitioned the Wake County Department of Education and demanded that her Cherokee children be sent to the local school and the superintendent agreed.

My brother and I stayed in the schools closest to our house for the remainder of our K-12 education and I didn't think any more of it. Yet after my mother died and I was cleaning out the closet under the stairs, I came upon a manila envelope with all the letters my mother wrote to the school district over the years. She petitioned for us to stay at our schools annually. It was a labor of love to keep her children closer to home and I doubt she was thinking it would have any influence on college.

When I was admitted to UNC-Chapel Hill in 1984, it wasn't a huge surprise. I had decent grades, and I demonstrated a significant increase in my GPA once I started dating our future high school valedictorian. What can I say? Love inspires. But the 2019 "Varsity Blues" college admission scandals got me thinking. Did my transcript say I was Native American? That must be how I got on the University's list of potential members of the American Indian Club? Is *that* the main reason that I was admitted? Am I an academic fraud?

But wait, it gets worse. My dad's sisters did 23andMe genetic testing and the results revealed that we have less than one percent Cherokee Indian in our DNA. That pride I long felt over having the blood of the original Americans coursing through my veins has been a sham. I am not at all who I thought I was.

In the end, I know that mothers will do whatever it takes for their children. I know my mother didn't lie. My father only knew what he'd been told about his own heritage, and there were no DNA tests back then. There also wasn't Photoshop so no one manipulated my face atop a Cherokee dancer at the Oconaluftee Village. No one faked my test scores or bribed a coach. I know *where* I am from, but I am left wondering *who* am I from.

CHAPTER FORTY-TWO
In The Air Tonight

I was not a summer-camp kid. I'd never shared a bunk bed in a cabin by a lake singing campfire songs or telling ghost stories. I dreamed of going to Camp Little Wolf like Tatum O'Neal and Kristy McNichol in *Little Darlings*, but instead I got to go pickup-truck camping with my whole family piled on a twin mattress in the metal truck bed, or make pillow-fort tents in the den while watching my younger siblings when my parents were out.

I'd only been away from home for occasional sleepovers, a luxury I always tried to arrange at the air-conditioned houses of my more affluent friends as often as possible in the summer. If friendship applications were a thing, mine would have included a box to check on temperature of sleeping quarters, and perhaps one on the number of younger siblings.

You see, I was not an only child, but I longed to be. My house was loud and I rarely recall an occasion when I was alone at home. By the time I was a young teen, we had four kids in our three-bedroom house. When my middle sister was a baby, my parents converted Mom's closet into a bedroom. The sliding louvered doors were removed, and Dad covered the space with Amish country-inspired red, white, and blue patriotic-patterned wallpaper. Itty-bitty baby dresses hung on one end of the rod above the crib and a mobile hung at the other end, with diapers and blankets lining the shelves. My mother's clothes were squeezed into one half of my father's tiny closet.

By the time that sister outgrew her crib, Mom was pregnant with another baby, and my brother was moved into the laundry room downstairs. Meager as it was, I fought hard for that space because there was a door leading to the backyard and I was already plotting my escape. I think we flipped a coin for that narrow little room, but clearly the toss was rigged. My parents would never intentionally let their daughters sleep near an exit.

I finally departed the nunnery when I went to college just thirty minutes from home, and the world opened up to me. But yet again, my space was crowded. The campus was behind in constructing new dorms, so they put three girls in rooms meant for two. Thankfully, my roommate's dad built us a loft to hold our three mattresses. It was totally campy and made our cramped space seem a lot more spacious. But the loft was also quite creaky. When Catherine or Stacy came home at 2 a.m. from a fraternity party before one of my 8 a.m. tests, the loft groaned on their ascent. Even though I was a Communications major, I never said anything. I surely also woke them up after a night or three spent out on Franklin Street. We just learned to live with the annoyances of incompatible schedules, or else we stewed in the frustrations.

As the school year stretched on and the bolts loosened, we were all sleep-deprived. And oh, how those rungs judged me like my mother with "Catholic creaks" when I climbed the ladder with Glen, the baseball center fielder I'd been waving at for months from the ninth-floor balcony as he headed toward Boshamer Stadium for practice. But at eighteen, I was determined to wait until I was married before having sex. Glen didn't want to keep climbing the ladder for no payoff and he soon stopped waving back.

One of my roommates once casually mentioned that she wanted to lose her virginity to her high school boyfriend while listening to Phil Collins' "In the Air Tonight." The song was number 19 on the "Billboard Top 100" that year, but it was already beginning to feel cliché to me. Everyone everywhere turned their steering wheels into snare drums, dorm desks into tom-toms, or drummed at the air while listening to cassettes through foamy headphones as if they were Phil rocking the solo in the quad.

One night, when I was sound asleep in my corner of the loft, I awoke to giggles and slurpy suction-cup kisses, the bang of a back against a closet door, louder laughter, and then the protest of the ladder. And yes, that would have been the time to announce my presence, but I didn't, because before I could clear my head of the cobwebs of sleep, I heard the click of the cassette deck and then the drum and cymbals…da da da da da chi, da da da da da chi…and Phil starts singing:

I can feel it coming in the air tonight
Oh, Lord

OH LORD! I hit my head on the ceiling as I popped up to plot my escape, but my route was blocked by the shadow of a naked boyfriend, and within moments the whole loft began rocking and groaning and there was rocking and groaning from a twin mattress mere feet away as I buried myself under my Laura Ashley comforter. Would they notice if I slid to the end of my mattress and slithered down the ladder like the Grinch taking a candy cane from Cindy Lou Who?

No, you don't fool me
Well, the hurt doesn't show
But the pain still grows
It's no stranger to you or me

And then the climactic drum roll and the, well, climactic roll. And I remained silent. I never did tell what happened in the air between the loft and the dorm room ceiling the night of my inadvertent threesome. I was a Communications major who just didn't have the words.

CHAPTER FORTY-THREE

Unspooled

W hen I was in college, I was addicted to collecting free or swiped items for my dorm room, which featured ashtrays and shot glasses pilfered from the college-town bars in Charlottesville and Winston-Salem when we followed our Tar Heels to football games on crisp fall days; road trips that are a blur of crashing on couches and wandering brick pathways, scanning ivy-covered quads to see if the Cavaliers or Demon Deacons had cuter boys than those in Chapel Hill.

As I stuffed a lowball glass from Third Edition in Georgetown into my purse and we posed for photos as if we were the cast from *St. Elmo's Fire*, I likely thought my thievery would demonstrate my willingness to take risks to my cute male accomplices. Being adventurous and fun-loving seemed to be more important than being an intellectual seeker of knowledge.

A boy who was clearly trying impress me once showed up at my dorm-room door with the Miller Light neon sign I'd admired the night before at Trolls, the basement bar with the sticky, beer-soaked floor. Sadly for him, the sign lit up my room, but I never gave him the chance to light up my life.

One evening as I walked across campus with my friends Ty and Randy after our first session in the basement computer lab, we noticed the open window on the second floor of the iconic, domed Wilson library. It was late and no one else was around because the dot-matrix printer had taken so long to spit out my essay on apartheid for my South African History class. I decided computers were stupid and I'd stick with my IBM Selectric typewriter with its white-out ribbon.

Renovations on the 1920s library had begun just before we started our freshman year. It was one of the prettiest buildings on campus—at least from the outside—but we weren't allowed inside. For all the money we were spending on tuition—I'd worked all summer selling ties and boxer shorts in the men's department at Ivey's to shell out $429 hard-earned dollars to cover my tuition that semester!—should they really be able to keep us out of a building *we* were paying for?

The thing about scaffolding is that it begs to be climbed. And the thing about second-floor windows that are open is that they beg to be climbed through.

We decided that the next night, we would host a séance in the scaffold-covered ancient library. Maybe bring back the ghosts of Thomas Wolfe or President Polk.

Reverent in the mission of our hastily formed secret society, the next evening Ty carried a bucket of bones from the local fried-chicken establishment, Time Out, like it was myrrh from a king. Those greasy bones were indeed a poor, drunk man's gold. Just 50¢ for an extra-large, popcorn-sized tub of chicken bones hugged by tiny pieces of meat that didn't make it onto a biscuit. Time Out was the place to be at 2 a.m. after the bars closed, when tipsy college kids needed something to soak up the alcohol. Nothing did the trick like a chicken biscuit. But if you didn't have a couple of bucks and were lucky enough to be in line at just the right time, a bucket of bones was the crack peddled by Billy Ray, the old guy working the fryer who handed them over with gusto, always a smile on his face as he laughed at the beer-soaked antics of his regulars and rapped his favorite song:

My name is Billy Ray and I'm here to say,
I'm gonna fry you some chicken.
I work at Time Out and I'm here to shout
that it's finger lickin'.

Now, I was a new vegetarian, having given up meat for Lent my freshman year after reading Upton Sinclair's *The Jungle* and Peter Singer's *Animal Liberation*. Surprisingly, giving up meat was a lot easier than giving up chocolate and made me feel far more enlightened.

In spring of sophomore year, Ty and Randy had joined us on a road trip to Annandale, Virginia where we stayed with my room-mate Krissy's family so we could be part of Hands Across America on the National Mall for my twentieth birthday. One afternoon, the guys asked us, "What's for lunch?" as if we were their private chefs. Well screw that! We made them canned dog-food sand-wiches, giggling as they devoured their meals. But I nearly gagged at the thought and extended my vegetarianism for decades. That wasn't so easy to do in the mid-1980s while living in the land of BBQ, sausage rolls and hamburger casseroles, at a time when a "gardenburger" was nothing but an oxymoron. I found myself eating a lot of house salads with jaw-breaking croutons.

Under the scaffolding of Wilson library, Ty passed the bucket of bones up to Randy, who was first up the scaffold tower. Whitney passed up the Ouija board and I climbed up with my backpack filled with candles and a picnic blanket. Eight of us slipped through the eighteen-inch window opening. Cobwebs and dust covered the empty mahogany shelves and card cata-logues. Our voices echoed off the stone columns and marble floors. MeriKay, who we were sure was destined to become an MTV VJ, passed around a joint as I lit the candles in a circle and Randy pulled wine coolers and beers from his satchel. Our séance devolved into laughter before we were able to conjure any spirits. At some point in the gale of guffaws, Randy pointed at a huge, empty copper-wire spool and said, "That would make a great bar!"

"We could totally put our Betamax on it," I said, and began to covet deeply the huge pine spool, imagining how I would surprise my unsuspecting roommate with this perfect gift. Then, as good friends do, mine commenced to plan the heist. We stuffed our bottles, bones and candle nubs into our backpacks and opened the window we'd entered as wide as it could go.

As we rolled the huge copper-wire spool out the second-floor window of Wilson Library, we felt like Robin Hood, taking from the rich to make a table and a bar for the poor. The cable reel landed on the brick sidewalk with a thud and Randy prevented it from rolling down the hill in the shadows while making sure the echoes of the fall didn't attract campus police. When we were in the clear, the rest of us shimmied down the stone wall of the library, hanging from the windowsill before dropping between the boxwood bushes below.

We rolled the giant spool down the brick-covered walkway, past the belltower, past Kenan Stadium, through the woods, and up the steep hill to Morrison dorm just as a campus police officer pulled up to the entrance.

"What do you kids think you're doing?" he called out. But we just rolled the spool faster into the lobby as MeriKay pushed the elevator button ten times in a second.

"Hey!" he shouted, following us. "Where did you get that?"

The elevator door closed before he could reach us.

We laughed all the way up, stopping at the seventh, eighth and ninth floors to throw the officer off the scent before rolling the spool into the tenth floor lobby, through the door of our suite, and then into room 1045, where it soon became the home to our television and Betamax player, which, when Blockbuster opened the following year, made our room the place to be to watch *Cheech & Chong*, *The Karate Kid* and *Sixteen Candles*. The lower shelf of the spool was filled with Everclear, Bacardi and Jägermeister, as we often were, too.

Decades later, when I finally went back to the campus and ventured into the venerable library filled with rare books and Southern historical collections, I walked over to the window from which, once upon a time, a wooden spool descended. I recalled the girl with the misdirected attentions and the oft misunderstood intentions, all the couldas, the wouldas, and the shouldas, and I knew I'd do it all again. Because the memories speak volumes and those volumes could fill a library.

CHAPTER FORTY-FOUR
Medicine Man

My roommate sophomore year and I were packing for another Spring Break in Daytona Beach when Krissy's parents called.

"Listen," her father said. "Our friend Fred has to have surgery on Monday and we've already got plane tickets and rooms lined up for a trip to the British Virgin Islands. He and Nancy can no longer go. Would you two like to join us?"

What this meant was we would have to head north to Baltimore from Chapel Hill that evening instead of south to Florida the following morning. Instead of driving in a caravan listening to mix cassettes en route to a Quality Inn along Atlantic Avenue, sleeping six to a room during Daytona's infamous Bike Week and subsisting on cheap beer and happy hour taquitos, we'd be flying to an island in the Caribbean. We'd jam to reggae music, stay at a luxury resort, and drink rum punch while eating plantains and pasteles in restaurants with ocean views.

Krissy and I talked about letting down our friends who were counting on our gas money and contributions to the kegs. We discussed how much we'd miss the biker gangs revving their engines on International Speedway Blvd. just outside our motel window at four a.m., and the cars cruising across the sand on Ormond Beach just feet from our towels. We wouldn't get to dance in a swirl of beer spray and tanning oil with college kids from across the Eastern seaboard while Eddie Money crooned "Two Tickets to Paradise" in a rumpled white linen suit without a shirt on a stage by the Main Street Pier. We weighed the pros and cons of joining her parents on a tropical island....

No we didn't. We said yes immediately and took off for Maryland within the hour.

I'd never been on a plane before, and my heart pounded with fear flying over a vast ocean with no place for an emergency landing. And it raced with excitement over this important step for not mankind, but my kind—the kind whose family could only afford camping trips without tents and borrowed beach trailer vacations. And while Krissy's parents settled into first class, their friends' nonrefundable tickets seemed to have been downgraded as we made ourselves comfortable in the Eastern Airlines' "smoking section" at the back of the plane and used our fake IDs to order the first of countless rum punches. The rectangular marks of the ashtray were branded into my palm as I intently gripped the armrest during the bumpy touch down at the Luis Muñoz Marín Aeropuerto in Puerto Rico. As we descended the stairs onto the tarmac, I breathed in the coconut scents mixed with jet fuel, a welcome relief from the Carlton 100s our seatmate puffed continuously for 1400 of the 1500 miles between our nation's capital and the British Virgin Islands.

Next, we boarded Air BVI to Tortola. This plane had just ten seats and we had to duck our way down the narrow aisle to get into them. The tiny vessel roared to life like a collection of tin cans being dragged behind a jalopy bearing a *Just Married* sign, and I reinforced my grip on my arm rests as we rose into the cloudless blue sky. When I dared to look out the window, I saw the cerulean sea dotted with reefs and tiny scrub islands speckled with palm trees. We glided over Sir Francis Drake Channel and landed on Beef Island forty-five minutes later. Our taxi took us over the

Queen Elizabeth II Bridge on the short trip to Road Town, and as we wound down the bougainvillea-lined drive to Prospect Reef Resort, I thought perhaps I was in a dream. When we walked into our room overlooking the lush gardens, I was fairly sure my plane had indeed gone down and I'd gone to heaven. I'd never had my own bed on vacation before. My family of six would stay in a single motel room with my parents in one bed and me and my middle sister in the other. We'd have a rollaway brought in for my brother while my parents pushed two chairs together to create a place for my youngest sister to sleep. Sometimes they would make my brother and me duck down in the back of the Ford Aerostar so they'd only be charged for a family of four. Then we'd hide under cover of the night behind Winn Dixie bags stuffed full of our clothing, flip flops, and sunscreen, and slip into our chlorine-scented home away from home.

But here, on the island, I had found paradise. At Brisani's we ordered Pina Coladas in coconut shells. We spent our first few days sailing to St. Thomas and Drake's Anchorage in Virgin Gorda with Krissy's parents, snorkeling in Loblolly Bay, and dancing at the hotel club where Krissy's mom was crowned limbo champ. It was lovely. But we were nineteen, and this was Spring Break. We decided to venture out of bounds because fun is generally never found within boundaries.

Walking along Waterfront Road, we came upon a thatched-roof bar with a live reggae band. There we found ourselves surrounded by college students all the way from Iowa and Missouri and others from Yale and Harvard. A group of Aussies mentioned a "medicine man" living in the hills overlooking Sea Cows Bay and, after several boozy Cruzan Confusions, we agreed to check it out with our newfound friends.

We piled into Sebastian's rust-orange Chevy Chevette and headed up the rugged dirt road. Sebastian was from Sydney and

had lived on Tortola for six months. He wore early-stage dreadlocks in his dust-colored hair and he smelled of cigarettes and
sun-dried sweat, but his accent was enchanting and I bumped
along in the backseat, hanging on every word.

Amani the medicine man's home was part shack, part tree
house. He sat on a wooden rocking chair under a guava tree,
clearly stoned out of his mind. Or maybe he just had crazy
eyes to go with his Medusa head of wild boa constrictor–sized
dreadlocks. He made Sebastian's dreads look like gently wound
spaghetti. Krissy and I shared glances, trying to play it cool
as Sebastian and his friends casually chatted with the mildly
deranged drug dealer. Our antennae were up and we sobered
up, fake-sipping the guavaberry wine he offered us as we came
to realize how stupid we were to accompany guys we didn't know
to a remote home without telling anyone where we had gone.

Fifteen dollars. We spent fifteen dollars on a film canister
crammed full of weed. Having never personally purchased pot
before, we considered our money well spent. Thankfully, with
the transactions complete, the Australians were ready to leave.

As we rode down the mountain with its spectacular view of
the sun setting beyond Nanny Cay, I breathed a pot-filled sigh
of relief. Krissy and I spent the last few days on Tortola trying
to use as much of our canister of cannabis as we possibly could
while hanging out with our new Aussie friends on the beach in
Smuggler's Cove. But try as we may, we were unable to make
much of a dent in our Kodak canister from the jungle dwelling
medicine man. As starving college students, we hated wasting
our money, so Krissy contrived a plan. As we waited for the taxi
to take us to the airport, she hid the container in her father's
suitcase, buried amidst his boxer briefs. What were the chances,
she reasoned, that anyone would think her jovial, bald, teetotal-
ing father was a drug smuggler? My fear of flying was overridden

by my fear that our reckless scheme would be thwarted and her poor dad would be sent to Rikers Island.

As we approached the airport, there were police officers with menacing dogs on leashes by the entrance of the tiny terminal. The cab driver piled our bags on a luggage cart and Krissy's dad smiled and nodded as he strolled past security and headed toward the ticket counter. The dogs didn't follow. Krissy and I locked eyes with relief and watched from the observation deck as our bags were loaded into the underbelly of the propeller plane.

When we landed in Baltimore that evening, Krissy somehow snuck our stash from her father's suitcase and the next day we headed back to Chapel Hill with a stop in Georgetown for a couple bottles of Everclear and Bacardi. After all, the drinking age was eighteen in that college town, and we were feeling invincible.

CHAPTER FORTY-FIVE
Con Job

J oe stepped out of the camper while popping the top on a can of Goebel that had clearly been shaken, the foam cascading across his wrist and landing on the Astroturf-covered patio like a blob of L'Oréal hair mousse.

Joe's stringy hair was tied back into a greasy ponytail that hung midway down his back. As he racked the pool balls, I noticed the black grit caked under his nails from his job at the auto mechanic shop. He announced that he and Dewey were a team if Brett and I dared to take them on. I stunk at pool and they all knew it, but they probably liked my Daisy Duke shorts so they let me hang out on the carport-turned-pool hall.

Brett had been my friend for years. Our families went to the same church, which was likely why my mother never questioned me hanging out at his house, even on a school night. We probably told her we were doing homework together, but I don't think Brett was ever in any of my honors classes and I doubt we ever opened a book. Mom certainly didn't know that my associates, Joe and Dewey, were ex-cons in their twenties and were living in the camper on the Marriott's driveway. Now, some might call that charitable. Mrs. Marriott clearly had a big heart. I don't know what relationship these guys had with the family and I have no idea what they did to land in jail. It was probably something like disorderly conduct or stealing a six-pack from the convenience store owned by a guy named—no joke—Jack Daniels, but I liked to imagine they were dangerous criminals and I was a daring accomplice, desperate to make my life more interesting than it was. I pretended that I was hanging out with Johnny and Henry from *The Sting*, only I wished they looked like Redford and Newman. In reality they more closely resembled a young Mr. Roper from *Three's Company* and Walter Matthau as Oscar in *The Odd Couple*.

Eventually, Joe and Dewey and their camper moved on. Brett joined the military, and I went off to college. But it was Joe and Dewey who came to mind when I found myself in handcuffs junior year. I went home for Thanksgiving and found a pile of mail stamped in red with *Urgent* and *Last Notice*. As I tore open the envelopes, postmarked in September and October, I quickly learned that I'd bounced a number of checks, apparently having deposited all my work income into my savings account. I ran downstairs.

"Mom! Why didn't you tell me I had mail marked urgent!"

"If you'd come home more often, you'd have known," she said, guilt dripping from every word.

As the gravy was passed around the Thanksgiving table, my mind was elsewhere, wondering how I'd dig my way out of my latest dilemma. I knew I'd have to go to my bank when I got back to school, pay the fines with my limited funds, then set out to restore my credit. What I didn't expect were the police officers outside my suite on the top floor of our dorm as soon as I returned, my backpack loaded with the final exams notes I'd spent very little time on over the four-day weekend, my suitcase full of clean clothes and food stolen from my parents' pantry. I'd justified that theft with the knowledge that if my original crime cost me very much money, I'd have nothing left to buy lunch.

Naturally, the elevator stopped at all nine floors heading down and I stood there in a sweaty panic as classmates, fellow resident assistants, and parents dropping their children off after the holiday looked on quizzically or with amusement from the common room lobbies as the elevator doors opened and police officers stood on opposite sides of the tenth floor RA, praying someone would get in to help break the tension, but hoping it wouldn't be anyone I knew.

"So, how was your Thanksgiving?" I asked the barrel-chested man in blue on my left. Small talk is my go-to.

"Had to work," he muttered, not making eye contact.

"Are you into canned or homemade cranberry sauce?" I asked the policewoman with the tight black bun on my right.

"I don't eat cranberry sauce," she replied as the doors opened on the floor with the mural saying *The Joy of Six,* where a couple of parents in Christmas tree sweaters opted to wait for the next elevator and not to help break the tension.

Now, I'd read that if ever you are kidnapped, you should try to make a connection so they see your humanity, so I kept going.

"Crazy that my mom has been holding my mail for months even though it was marked urgent," I said as we stopped on the third floor.

"Tell it to the judge," said Officer Cranky as he straightened his holster.

The elevator opened again, and there on three stood my crush from the soccer team with five fellow players, heading to the training table, no doubt, where the food was rumored to be far superior than any campus dining hall. None of the players moved forward to join us once they saw the officers standing alongside the obviously dangerous criminal in a gray Fetzer Gym sweatshirt that they were escorting. Donald clearly recognized the criminal just as the doors closed and my wrists strained at the handcuffs wanting to wave, give a peace sign, or some indication that I was still dateable.

By now, half of the nine hundred students living in my dorm had gathered on the southern balconies to see why there was a police cruiser with flashing lights on Manning Drive, and they all witnessed officers Cranky and Cranberry open the door and guide one of Morrison Dorm's RAs into the car with a hand on the top of my head.

I sat in a jail cell for a couple hours next to a woman from Durham who was arrested for driving under the influence. She was clearly still quite drunk as she slurred her story of innocence a little too close to my face, her breath a mixture of rubbing alcohol and pepperoni pizza.

"Why you here, sweetie?" she asked as she brushed a tangle of what I now saw as vomit-crusted hair out of her eyes with her red chipped fingernails.

"Murder," I said flatly, which had the effect I desired as she slid to the far end of the bench.

"Well goddamn! I never would have guessed that." Despite some furtive glances, she soon fell into a snore-filled slumber.

What would Joe and Dewey do? I thought as I pondered my escape and contemplated getting kicked out of college for being a convicted criminal and having to live in a camper in the driveway of a charitable neighbor.

My friend Bill picked me up twenty minutes after I was given a chance to make a phone call, and my case was heard first thing on Monday morning. The fine was a little over $100, which I paid with borrowed cash as they would not accept my checks. I made good with the bank fees later that day, moving all my savings into my checking account, and I was left with approximately $24.56 to my name. Ahh, but having a thousand fellow students wondering what you were arrested for and now being known as the bad girl? Priceless.

CHAPTER FORTY-SIX

God in The Trees

W̲e are sitting under a giant oak tree in Polk Place, the proverbial tree-lined quad that stretches from the domed Wilson Library to the old brick South Building in the middle of UNC-Chapel Hill's picturesque campus. The dogwoods and azaleas are in bloom and the sky is the Carolina blue that is said to be proof that God is a Tar Heel.

Professor Kaufman is perfectly cast in this scene with his five o'clock shadow at eleven o'clock in the morning, wire-rim glasses and rumpled khaki pants. He is sitting cross-legged as we gather in a circle on the ground, some perched on the bulging roots of the ancient oak. He is about to reveal the truth of the universe and every pore in my body is alert. This is it. This is why I came to college: so that I can understand the deepest questions that confront humanity.

Our Religions of Man professor is dynamic, brilliant and engaging. He paces across the lecture hall talking with authority about the tenets of Judaism, Islam, Hinduism, Sikhism and Christianity. He is a religion rock star and he looks a bit like Rick Springfield, who I am also sure is a gift from God.

Students beg him to share his personal beliefs and he demurs, eventually promising that he will share his perspective on religion on the last day of class. I harbor a deep hope that this man of great wisdom will agree with my mother. She maintains that she has never questioned what she learned in church. She is absolutely, resolutely certain that what her long, multi-generational Irish Catholicism taught her is 100 percent true. Period. Full stop.

But I have questions. So many questions. Bible passages confuse me. Countless things that our priest says make no sense. When I ask Mom about them, she says, "In God's will there is great faith." To her, the Bible is the definitive "word of God." But aren't parables just stories? If humans wrote these tales and humans are fallible, how do you know what is true?

When I was fifteen and preparing for my confirmation, I asked the priest why it was that we Catholics believe all the tenets of the Apostles' Creed and how we know what is actually God's will.

"Because God tells us it is so," he said. "Ours is not to question; ours is just to trust."

"But why?" I got no answers to any of my questions. I was instead given penance for asking them.

And I did my penance, a shitload of Hail Mary's and Our Fathers, all which felt forced and disconnecting. But I went through with my confirmation, attesting that I believe all of that which makes no sense to me, mostly because I got a new dress and got to go out to eat with my family at Neptune's Galley to celebrate.

But now I don't really know what I believe. I feel guilty for not going to confession and for lying at my confirmation. I can't admit it to anyone, but the lack of thoughtful answers pokes at my brain like a crown of thorns. The priest. My mother. I've tried to be honest about my concerns, but no one seems to care or have answers save for "that is why it is called faith, because you believe that for which there is no proof."

Yet as Professor Kaufman stands at the podium in a nondescript lecture hall, I am drawn into the possibility that there are other ways to see God, and if he exists, maybe he isn't as wrathful as I'd been led to believe. Maybe hell and damnation aren't my destiny for my uncertainty. Maybe he is a she? Somewhere in between samsara and Shalom, I determine that whatever the scholarly and astute Dr. Kaufman says on our last day of school will be part of the answer that will guide my life.

On Sundays, I often go to Mass at the Newman Student Center, perhaps to maintain some connection to my upbringing and to have something to share with my mother that will make her happy on our weekly Sunday evening calls, but mainly because of all the hot lacrosse, baseball and soccer players from Yankee Catholic families who regularly attend. I dress piously hot—as in, I wear my confirmation cross along with a hint of cleavage and take communion with a reverence that makes it clear I'd be the kind of girlfriend they can proudly bring home to meet their mother.

On the last day of class, we sit with the dappled light of the oak tree dancing in Professor Kaufman's luscious hair, and he gazes up toward the heavens and takes a deep breath, then looks us all in the eyes, and says, "When I look at this tree and all of the beauty in the nature that surrounds us on this campus, I am quite certain that it was not created by any ethereal being called God." And I now know in my heart what I think I always knew. Still, I am sad.

CHAPTER FORTY-SEVEN
Changes in Latitudes, Changes in Attitudes

I always knew I would go to college, even though I would be the first in my family to do so. I just never expected to be contemplating dropping out to sail to Jamaica with a possible drug smuggler.

You see, at twenty years old, I longed to see the world, but when I presented brochures about studies abroad in Rome, Paris, or a Semester at Sea, they were flatly rejected by my parents. "Where are you going to find the money for that?" Mom asked, knowing that I could barely cover my bills as it was. I started babysitting at ten, and by thirteen I was making a whopping $2 an hour watching the demonic five-year-old twins up the street.

Let's review my work resume: hanging clothes and stocking shelves at T.J. Maxx, offering soup or salad plates to customers in line at Golden Corral, hand modeling for Black + Decker where my boss told me to make drill bits seem sexier, and selling housewares, junior clothing and men's ties at Ivey's. I should probably have gone home for Spring Break junior year and worked at my department store job, but I made an impressive $50 donating plasma, which was far less painful than babysitting the Shining twins. I figured those $50 bucks could easily last me for a week in the Florida Keys. I knew my only hope for adventure was seizing opportunities as they presented themselves.

So, off I go with a car full of friends down I-95 with our only two cassettes, Van Halen's *5150* and Dire Straits' *Brothers in Arms* on repeated rewind, but our planned fifteen-hour trip becomes much longer after we spend several hours at a rural Georgia gas station getting a blown tire fixed by a lanky dude named Possum who had two months of motor oil caked under his nails and two days of tobacco tucked under his lower lip. A red plastic Georgia Bulldogs cup filled with juicy brown spittle is balanced precariously on his toolbox. He insists that "Possum" is his real name, not a nickname. The whole scene would have been a great ad for why you should always carry a working spare tire and pepper spray.

We finally arrive at our rented bungalow in Key West around two a.m., totally exhausted, and fall asleep wherever we find space. It is raining the first morning when I wake up and climb out of a top bunk, navigating the suitcases and bodies buried in sleeping bags covering the floor, unsure which one is my college roommate and which is her best friend from UVA.

I tiptoe to the kitchen where I'm greeted by a pile of pizza boxes, bongs and beer bottles blanketing all flat surfaces. On the L-shaped couch in the living room, two guys are passed out like starfish with arms and legs draped over the cushions. I pour orange juice into a hopefully unused Solo cup and quietly sneak out to the screened-in porch to take in the rain. It's coming down hard. Puddles surround the palmetto plants that line the walkway to the bungalow where nineteen twenty-year-olds are sleeping in a rental meant for nine. Life is goooooooooood.

I hear rustling and mumbled dialogue from inside the house.

"Oh crap!" whines a female voice. "It's raining! Now what are we supposed to do?"

I hear the sound of a beer tab popping open. "Hair of the dog, am I right?" grunts one of the guys.

"Anyone seen my bag of weed?" asks another male.

A girl starts panicking. "I needed to start my base tan today! Our Spring Break is ruined!"

My best friend Cathy stumbles out to the porch, her hair a comical nest of tangles. She grabs my Solo cup and takes a big swig of juice. "No vodka?" she jokes. "We need to get away from this bunch. They're too negative."

We pull t-shirts over our bikini tops, tie our hair into scrunchies and link arms as we skip down the broken flagstone pathway like Dorothy and the Scarecrow heading toward the Emerald City. We soon find ourselves soaked and giggling under the limited cover of palm trees outside the already bustling bar, Sloppy Joe's. It's ten a.m. And already it's pretty obvious why it's called Sloppy Joe's.

With our flip-flops squishing, we plop ourselves on barstools.

"Two slices of Key Lime pie and two Rum Runners please," Cathy says, ordering our "breakfast of champions" as thunder booms in the distance. We breathe in the scent of salty sea and petrichor and take in Papa's Wall filled with photos of Hemingway, who once said "There's no friend as loyal as a book." I look at Cathy and know in my heart that she's the exception. She still is.

We are plotting our return to the bar later that afternoon for live music when a deeply tan middle-aged woman on the barstool next to us says, "Ya'll look like fun!"—her thick southern accent made all the thicker by what I'm sure wasn't her first Piña Colada of the day. A man with faded tattoo sleeves comes up and wraps his arms around her. We have no idea who these people are, yet we hang out with them for a while and then they ask if we'd like to join them and their new friend for a boat ride.

"Sure!" we say. The sun is just beginning to break through and we have nothing better to do, and we're too naïve and full of Rum Runners to think this is probably the perfect meet and greet for deranged serial killers.

We head to the dock and follow the pair to a teak-sided sailboat.

"Hey Jon!" the tanned woman calls out.

A man with dark curly hair pops out of the hull. "Eh, good to see ya! Ready for a ride?" he asks. His accent is like a joyful reggae refrain.

"We thought you wouldn't mind if we brought a couple friends?"

"The more the merrier. Hop aboard!"

It never dawns on us that none of our friends know where we are. Cathy's parents don't even know we're in Florida, and likely don't know it is Spring Break. They probably still think she's in her dorm. Had she asked, they'd have forbidden her to go, especially if they'd known there'd be boys on the trip. My parents only know I'm in the Keys with my college roommate and best friend. They didn't ask who else was going and I didn't share. As long as I didn't ask for money, it didn't really seem to matter what I was up to providing I called home collect and spoke really quickly on Sunday, when the rates were cheapest.

If our new friends are deranged killers, they are at least entertaining and beyond generous as we enjoy an endless flow of drinks, snacks and weed while Cat Stevens sings about it being a *Wild World*, and we're gleefully gliding on the water adjacent to the palm tree-dotted shore. Like typical stoned and silly college girls, we crack up every time someone mentions poop deck. I duck down to use the head and catch a glimpse of a drawer filled to the brim with plastic bags of ganja and imagine our college friends would love to get their hands on some of our good fortune.

Soon we pull up to a dock with a bar set up along the side to serve the two or three boats able to squeeze into the slip.

Jon orders bottles of champagne and platters full of Oysters Rockefeller and French fries. It is the grandest meal I've had in my life. Jon hands the waitress several crisp hundred-dollar bills and the other couple hops off. We figure we should as well, and get back to our friends. Jon offers to take us for a sail around Wisteria Island the next day. You can practically hear Keith Morrison from *Dateline* retelling the episode.

That evening, we are reunited with our college friends at a long table at Margaritaville when a mustachioed dude in a Hawaiian shirt joins the band. Before he even mentions *nibblin' on sponge cake*, we realize it is Jimmy Buffett and we all sing along at the top of our lungs. Sometimes life is simply magical.

Cathy is hungover when we arrive for our second day of sailing, and she gets seasick at the first sign of choppy waves. Jon pushes her into the water and declares, "That'll cure you!" without bothering to ask if she can swim. You would think that would have been a bit of a red flag but thankfully Cathy *can* swim, and it *did* cure her hangover. We snorkel for a while and it's beautiful, with Jon pointing out parrotfish, angelfish and spiny lobsters.

Jon is in his mid-thirties, so he's pretty old in our book, but he's a seasoned sailor, catching fish and then grilling them for lunch right on the deck. The ocean spray dances across our legs and I am devouring the possibilities of a future of decadence and excitement when Jon comes up from the galley carrying a joint the size of a cigar. The thick scent of Stuart Johnson's basement after a high school football game wafts over to where Cathy and I are bronzing ourselves on the deck, me in my high-waisted yellow and black bikini like a burnt bumble bee and Cathy like Sophia Loren, glamorous in a string bikini, her hair bouncing into natural waves after her dip in the Gulf Stream. In contrast, my hair dries like matted straw and I resemble Spicoli in *Fast Times at Ridgemont High*. Still, I am on a boat off the Florida coast, living the literal high life.

I sit up, squinting toward the cloud of smoke that briefly surrounds Jon before ocean breezes send it out to sea. He walks across the deck, wind in his curly hair, and passes the doobie to Cathy, who takes a deep drag. Bob Marley is singing *Could You be Loved* and rays of sunshine stream down from behind puffed cumulous clouds as if angels are shining a hundred spotlights on this stage that is our Spring Break in the tropics. I take a puff and a big swig of my Bartles & Jaymes wine cooler to stave off a coughing attack. Cathy has flipped onto her stomach and grabs a handful of Doritos, the caustic orange dust coating her fingertips as she sways to the rhythm of the music mixed with the rhythm of the waves.

We talk about where Jon is heading next.

"Back to Jamaica," he says, and he describes the rich flavors of jerk sauce and infectious ska rhythms, the friendly people and the breezy Island life. "It's like here only better," he says with a nostalgic lilt to his voice. "You should come with me," he suggests.

Maybe it is the marijuana taking the lead for my brain, but I tell him, honestly, that I'm considering it. If my dream in life is to see the world, why do I need to need a piece of paper proving I've completed a bunch of classes when I can go to the school of life? I could see the world in a way that goes deeper than anything in those stupid, glossy brochures or textbooks. This could be my study abroad! I could go back to school later. Maybe get a job in Jamaica, *mon*. I mean college is just a stressful mix of due dates and wondering how I'm going to pay my next bill. But this? This is life in technicolor, I think, as pelicans nosedive into the water and Jon, stoned as usual, free-climbs to the top of the mast and hangs off of it, laughing. And Cathy and I laugh too.

But when he starts doing acrobatic tricks like an exotic dancer on a stripper pole while the boat crashes against the waves and he's flying through the air with just one hand on the masthead, Cathy and I sober up quickly, realizing that we can't even see land at this point and if Jon falls, we have no idea what direction to go or how to sail a boat. It's not as if either of us has paid even a tiny bit of attention to any of the ship's mechanics, save for occasionally ducking as the boom swings toward us and nearly knocks our wine coolers from our hands.

Fortunately for us, Jon successfully shimmies back down the mast with the agility of a circus performer. He sees me shivering as we bounce across the waves, heavy mist splashing us in our perches on the stern. Ever the Jamaican gentleman, he pops into the galley, coming up with a red sweatshirt, and offers it to me.

As I pull it over my head, I realize I'd rather freeze. This thing reeks of body odor and as I pull it back off, I see that the fuzzy inside is covered in dark curly hairs. I decide right then and there that I cannot accompany Jon to Jamaica. It isn't that I'd have to drop out of school. It isn't that I hardly know him, or that he is very likely smuggling drugs. It is the lack of deodorant and the likeliness that his back and chest are covered in a carpet of hair that determines my fate to complete my college degree.

Now forty years later, I have traveled throughout North America and to many countries in Europe, but I still haven't been to Jamaica. The school of life has taught me that every experience informs some part of who we become—or at least gives us funny stories to reflect back on—but you have to keep pursuing a robust bucket list to keep life interesting and hopeful. Sometimes that bucket list can include board games with the family. It is time with the people we love that really makes our lives rich.

My best friend and I still use Key West as the barometer against which we rate all adventures. Nothing was ever as reckless and nothing may ever be as delicious as oysters at sunset on a boat in the Keys, but I'm going to keep my eyes and heart open for the next adventure and the next laugh because:

> *Yesterday's over my shoulder, so I can't look back for too long*
> *There's just too much to see waiting in front of me and I know*
> *that I just can't go wrong*
> *With these changes in latitudes, changes in attitudes*
> *Nothing remains quite the same*
> *With all of my running and all of my cunning*
> *If I couldn't laugh I just would go insane.*
> *If we weren't all crazy we would go insane.*
> —Jimmy Buffett, *"Changes in Latitudes, Changes in Attitudes"*

CHAPTER FORTY-EIGHT
The Cow and the Birds

I am lying on a towel at Wrightsville Beach, drifting in and out of consciousness. Amazed that we actually did it. I did it! I did *it*. My skin is the copper tone I'd spent entire summers cultivating with baby oil and iodine throughout my teen years— and that I now regret as what was once smooth and bronzed is now creped and splotched with freckles and age spots. But back then and well into my twenties, I loved being golden brown.

So, there on my towel, the sea grass rustling ever so slightly in the occasional fall breeze, the sound of Starship's "Nothing's Gonna Stop Us Now" is coming from a boom box two or three beach umbrellas over, and I am afraid and amazed and excited and disappointed and somewhat impressed with myself because finally, after nearly twenty-one years on this planet, I am no longer a virgin. It didn't happen exactly as I'd intended, flower petals, candlelight and a memorable song playing on the turntable. But still, it finally happened!

My devout Catholic mother had done everything in her power to sabotage pretty much every relationship I'd had throughout high school and college, thinking that if I didn't get too close to a boyfriend, I'd never have sex with one.

"Well, you went to the prom with him last year, honey, don't you think you should go out with a different boy for homecoming? Play the field a bit? You're too young to settle down!" She'd subtly mention faults with the boys I'd bring home, casually planting seeds I'd never notice were blooming until hindsight revealed her cunning gardening.

Mom believed absolutely in abstinence until marriage and I had found that to be a helpful mantra in many teen and early college relationships, or when I wasn't sure about a boy. It proved to be an easy way to weed out the ones who "were just after one thing," as my mother assured me they all were. "They won't buy the cow if they can get the milk for free," she often said, suggesting, it seemed, that as a cow, my main goal should be to give my milk only to the one who owned me.

As the semesters of college rolled by, I struggled with my inner desires and that albatross of chastity that I wasn't so sure I agreed with any longer. I mean, I didn't plan to get married any time soon. I wanted to travel! I wanted a career! I longed for adventure! I had no idea when Mr. Right would show up in this future that was spread out before me like the K&W cafeteria buffet.

So, I came up with a plan. A mental *trompe l'oeil*, if you will. I decided that I would wait until I was twenty-one. The same age my mother was when she lost her virginity in Niagara Falls on her honeymoon when she got pregnant with me. I had seven months to go.

I had a boyfriend that I liked fairly well. We'd been dating for a few months and so far he hadn't balked at not having sex. I hadn't told him about the plan that was percolating in my head. So, when he came to my dorm room one Friday afternoon and we were fooling around in my twin bed, somehow my guard was down and caution was thrown to the wind as the condom wrapper was thrown to the floor and we just…did it. And I was surprised by myself, but not as surprised as I was by the first words out of his mouth mere moments later: "Oh shit! I have to go! I'll be late for work!" He kissed me on the forehead and said he loved me as he pulled on his pants and rushed out the door.

He called later that night to say he'd gotten a friend's beach cottage for the weekend and he wanted to make it up to me. This time there would be candles and music. And there were. Roses, too. And breakfast in bed. It was a good effort and the sex, well, it was a little more memorable, though I wasn't sure if it was me or if it was him or if I just hadn't picked the right person.

So, there I was, several hours later, lying on a towel and contemplating this unexpectedly pivotal weekend, dozing in the surprisingly warm October sun. The nearby boom box may be playing Wang Chung or maybe it's Bruce Hornsby, but suddenly, whatever the song is, it is drowned out by the sounds of loud squawking, getting louder and louder and closer and closer by the second, and I peel open my eyes to see the sun blocked by birds diving right at me, surrounding me in a crazy Alfred Hitchcockian cacophony of wings and beaks and bird poop on my legs and in my hair. They are everywhere and I can't sit up for fear of being scratched by talons. I fold up into a ball, covering my face with my hands and pulling my towel partly over my shoulder and legs. And when the racket dies down to just an occasional *caw!* I am wondering if this is some kind of punishment from God for my terrible deed. I slowly roll over and look up to see my boyfriend laughing hysterically. He had poured a bag of potato chips in a circle around me, inciting the bird riot that left me feeling like Tippi Hedren, and I knew I really hadn't picked the right person.

The next time I gave that milk away for free, I was a lot smarter about it and I never again fell asleep on a beach towel.

CHAPTER FORTY-NINE
Motorcycle Diary

We rumbled into the driveway with the engine growling like a five-hundred-pound grizzly bear. It was both exhilarating and terrifying, my arms wrapped around my new boyfriend's waist as we flew down the highway from our college town toward my childhood home. I'd never been on a motorcycle until I found myself in this whirlwind romance. Mere months before college graduation, my sights were set not on my next career steps, but on how I could *carpe* the heck out of the next ninety *diems*. Riding on a Harley to the beach seemed like a great way to seize that day, but I couldn't pass by my home exit along the highway without stopping to at least say hello. And, of course, I've always liked making an entrance.

In my mind, I stepped off that motorcycle in the driveway wearing tight jeans and sexy boots and pulled off my helmet with a flourish, blonde hair cascading across my shoulders as my little sisters ran out to the driveway, awed by their cool older sister. In reality, I was probably wearing a college sweatshirt and tennis shoes and the removal of the helmet revealed sweaty, matted locks.

What I do remember with certainty, though, was the look on my mother's face as she stood in the doorway wiping her hands on her pink apron. She wasn't impressed. She didn't think me cool. Not only was I on a motorcycle, something she'd expressly forbidden when I was in high school, but I was with a boy she'd never met, on the way to the beach with no actual plan for where we were staying, which likely meant unacceptable and unladylike sleeping conditions.

"What are you thinking?" she hissed under her breath after she politely greeted my new beau with a forced smile. "You know I do *not* approve."

We made small talk and drank lemonade in the living room while my sisters snuggled under my armpits and I tried to avoid my mother's steely gaze.

"Don't make me have to say I told you so when you're broken and bloodied in a hospital bed," she muttered as I came out of the bathroom and knelt down to say goodbye to my sisters.

I rolled my eyes. "Come on, Mom. John's a safe driver."

Then she tried a different approach, tears welling in her eyes and a plea escaping from her pursed lips. "God saved you once. I don't know that you'll get another chance."

But I let the screen door slam behind me, invincible.

Yet Mom's motorcycle paranoia had a legitimate root.

To set the scene, you should know that my father was deep in the North Atlantic aboard the USS *Alexander Hamilton* when he heard the news of his first baby's birth in May of 1966. Dad had enlisted in the Navy straight out of high school. Had he not done so, he'd have been drafted about two months later and would likely have been a foot soldier in Vietnam. Instead, he was one hundred feet under water in a nuclear submarine off the coast of Norway monitoring the movements of the Russians.

The Baby-Gram delivered to the twenty-two-year-old cadet read: *Your wife gave birth to a 7 lb 6 oz baby girl. Both mother and newborn daughter are doing fine. RADM Laughlin and the Radio Gang send congratulations.*

My father had worked his way up to atmospheric analyzer by

his third year as a sailor. He was tasked with ensuring that the air quality and oxygenation was within the acceptable range during the sixty days that the ship was typically submerged. He took a deep breath. He was a father.

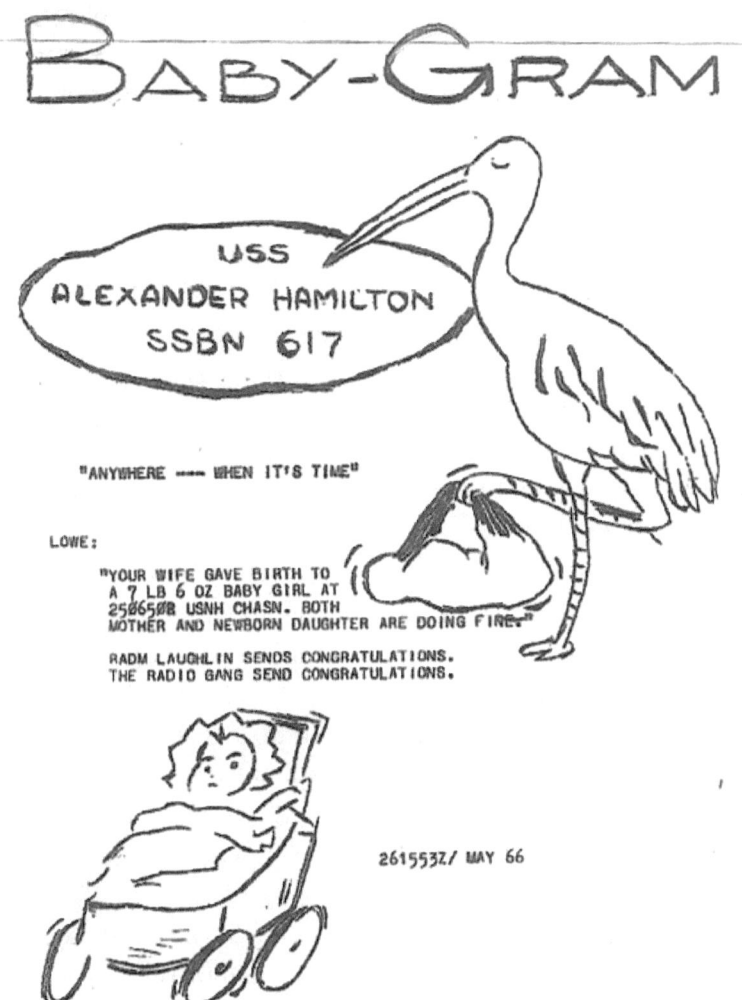

My twenty-one-year-old mother was in foreign lands herself. Born and raised in Brooklyn, she married my father while he was on shore leave, just after she graduated from nursing school. They honeymooned in Niagara Falls for a couple of nights, then headed to the Navy base in Charleston, South Carolina, from where he departed three days later for a six-month deployment. My mother had never been outside of New York when she moved to the land of sweet tea and mint juleps, and she was alone.

But she found work as a nurse in a hospital, using her hard-earned degree and keeping herself busy to push down the profound pangs of loneliness. Several months into her first job, she felt a little nauseous while on a pediatric shift and rushed to the bathroom down the hall from the nurse's station. As she was washing her hands, a toilet in an adjacent stall flushed and out came the head nurse, who told my mother she was pregnant before my mother realized it herself.

"Hospital work is no place for a woman with child," said her boss. "Your time would be wiser spent making a home for your husband and baby."

Three months after my mother began her career, it was over.

Toward the end of the pregnancy, my grandmother came down to the little brick house on Aldeen Avenue. For my mother, the birth was bittersweet without her new husband there. But the baby girl had all of her fingers and toes, though she was jaundiced and had to stay in the hospital for several days until the yellow-orange tint of her skin faded to a more normal rosy color. Additional checkups were ordered to ensure that the tiny baby's liver was functioning.

On the way home from one of those checkups, my mother and grandmother sat on the front bench seat of Mom's two-tone green 1964 Chevy Impala. The baby was in a plastic bassinet between them. There were no seat belts.

Several miles away, a sailor had just been discharged from the Navy after six years of commendable service. He'd been drinking all night before climbing onto his motorcycle, whiskey bottles clanking together in his saddlebags as he turned north onto Highway 52. But in his haze, he turned into the southbound lanes and was swerving in and out of oncoming traffic. He'd traveled several miles, narrowly avoiding the cars and big-rig trucks in his path, before police gave chase.

Mom could hear the sirens before she saw the police cars. And when she saw them many yards in the distance, she'd not yet noticed the motorcycle tearing across the asphalt in her direction. She pulled toward the shoulder and rolled to a stop, giving the motorcyclist more room to maneuver past. But he was barreling straight for her car at one hundred miles an hour. My grandmother put the baby in the carrier on the floor of the car between her legs and braced for impact. And it was like an explosion. A face coming straight at them. *Did he seem to be laughing?* No helmet. Her eyes squeeze shut. Breath held. Glass shatters as handlebars slam into the hood, propelling the sailor into the windshield as the bike flies through the air, landing ten yards away on the sandy shoulder.

The motorcyclist was dead on impact and later found to have LSD coursing through his system, along with the Jack Daniels. Blood dripped through the hole in the windshield. Fragments of glass stuck out of Grandma's arm and cheeks. Mom's face was bleeding from the force that slammed her backwards before her forehead smashed into the steering wheel. There were no airbags back then. And the baby?

"How's my baby?" Mom screamed.

The tiny girl was covered in glass. And she was silent. Not a sound. Grandma reached down to pick her up. A diaper pin had come loose and as Grandma lifted her, the baby peed all over the blood-covered bench seat.

A urine blessing, my mother thought. A second chance.

My dad found out about the accident when he met my mother and me while on shore leave three weeks later. I was the little yellow child once blanketed in glass who later cavalierly rode out of my parents' driveway under a blanket of stars, one of many times I tempted fate. I was determined no one would ever think me yellow. But bravery looks different in hindsight. My mother at twenty-one had a lot more guts than I'd ever had.

CHAPTER FIFTY

You've Lost That Lovin' Feeling

"I love you." Three simple words that can pop the bubble wrap around a heart, words that dreams are built upon, words that you might do stupid things to hear. In the case of Dan, I can't recall if we ever actually exchanged those words, but I know I felt it. Mad, crazy love. Reroute your path around campus for a just a glimpse of his smile kinda' love. And I think he felt it too. For a time.

But I should have known what was coming when I walked to Dan's dorm room the night before school closed for Christmas break, carrying his present wrapped in green foil paper and tied with a silver bow. We both had exams the next morning, but we'd planned a romantic pre-holiday dinner. I'd been thinking about our date for days: what I'd wear, where we might go, the sex afterwards. I'd planned my study schedule to ensure I was prepped for the final of my finals well in advance. I wanted to be fully present for my present. To me, no test was as important as the last night the two of us would be together for three whole weeks.

Dan had Paul Newman eyes, exotic Northeast sensibilities, a love of sports and a way with words. He told me once that he loved girls in pink and that the scent of Obsession perfume drove him crazy. He wrote a sports column for the college paper and I spent hours studying the rosters of his hometown teams so I could chime in when we watched football on Sundays at his fraternity house.

"Jim Kelly hasn't thrown like that since he was MVP in the Peach Bowl for Miami!" I'd casually throw into the conversation as I reached for a potato chip.

But that morning, Dan pushed our time back. Then he called a couple hours later to say he didn't think dinner would work after all. "Maybe we can just exchange gifts after the holidays?" he said a little too casually, as if the last three months weren't the best months of his life.

Well, I couldn't have that. "How about I come over now?" I suggested brightly. "I really want you to have your gift before you leave!"

And that was true. I needed for him to have the carefully framed collage of photos of us together so he could share our love with his family back in New York. There were images of us with our faces painted at the Duke football game, smiling arm in arm under the dome of the Old Well, and toasting at a table at Spanky's with our friends. I wanted to make sure he remembered that I was one of the best things about fall semester and would be the best thing about coming back in 1988.

So I showed up at his dorm wearing my newest pink-striped sweater and a healthy spritz of Obsession. Our hug was, well, not as affectionate as I might have liked. We sat on his twin mattress and I handed him his gift. He opened it and put it on his desk.

"You could bring it home," I suggested. "In case you miss me."

"Ok," he said rather flatly as he handed me my gift in an equally flat paper bag. "Sorry, I didn't have time to wrap it."

Clearly, it was a book. And when I opened it, I found a thin paperback with a pastel cover, a book of mediocre poems edited by Susan Polis Schultz. The kind of book you'd find at a car wash. *Don't Ever Give Up On Your Dreams* stated the title.

"Thank you," I said, feigning appreciation as my heart sank. My dream was Dan. His gift didn't mirror my feelings. This was not Wordsworth, Neruda or Keats. These were not love poems to span the ages. And it was clear we would not be curling up on his bed to read them together that night.

Dan needed to get back to studying, he said, and before I knew it, I was walking back to my dorm alone on a cold dark night, carrying only a sliver of hope in that sliver of a book in a brown paper bag. When I got home, I found the receipt from the drug store on Franklin Street. Not the bookstore. The drug store. $3. It was purchased around the time he cancelled our dinner date earlier that evening.

Christmas of 1987 was miserable. I spent most of my time staring at the phone, picking up the receiver periodically to see if it was still working. But Dan never called. A week went by. I baked cookies, sang carols, wrapped presents, played in the dusting of snow with my sisters, but I never strayed too far from the phone, just in case it rang and it was Dan.

At dinner one night, the phone did ring. But there was a rule in our house. No phone calls during dinner. And there was no answering machine. Mom never cared. "If they really want to reach us, they'll call back later." Dad was sure it was someone from work. "If it's important, they can call someone else," said Mom.

Maybe it was Publisher's Clearing House alerting us to our million-dollar check! Maybe it was an Encyclopedia salesman. Maybe it was Dan.

"Mom, please!" I pleaded.

But rules are rules. And the phone rang and rang. Unanswered phone calls in my youth were like unsolved mysteries. Surely if I'd answered, my relationship would have been saved.

Christmas Eve came and went. I played with my sisters and their American Girl dolls and sullenly listened to my new *Hysteria* and *Joshua Tree* cassettes on my Sanyo Walkman from Santa as the hours of Christmas day ticked by. Finally, I decided, it's a holiday and therefore totally appropriate and not at all needy for me to call Dan.

Heart pounding and hopeful that it was just that he was busy, what with a big Catholic family he'd not seen since August, I dialed slowly, willing Dan to answer. But a woman's voice came on the line.

"Merry Christmas!" she said brightly. There were voices in the background.

"May I please speak to Dan?"

"Oh honey, he stepped out for a bit. May I give him a message?"

"Yes, please." I tried to sound cheerful. "Just tell him Suzanne from Carolina called."

I hoped my name would sound familiar and perhaps this person who was likely his mother would say, "Oh! Suzanne! He can't stop talking about you." But there was no familiarity at all.

"Ok, will do. You have a nice evening, now." And the conversation was over. And Dan didn't call back.

Three days went by before I heard from Dan. Yes, the holidays were nice and yes, he'd been really busy with his friends and extended family and short trips into the city and how was I? Of course, I didn't share that I was miserable, that I missed him desperately because I didn't want to seem desperate. I feigned equivalent busy-ness and casually suggested we get together as soon as we're back at school and exactly when would that be for him?

We made a plan. My spirits lifted as I imagined seeing him mere hours after my return to campus in less than a week. I had renewed energy as I reconnected with my high school friends for New Year's Eve.

"Yeah, I have a boyfriend. He lives out of state," I shared with feigned confidence.

But then it was the first week of January and I was back in my dorm room, waiting. Dan was late and hadn't called. I finally reached him and he said he was heading over now. I fluffed up my hair and spritzed on a little extra Obsession and there was a knock and there was Dan, handsome as ever…and backed by three of his fraternity brothers. Before I could say anything, Dan filled in the space. "The guys wanted to join us. I told them you wouldn't mind." He'd brought backup. I did mind. I didn't say anything, though. I grabbed my coat and we all walked together to Four Corners, my favorite bar across from campus.

There I sat in the booth trying to catch Dan's eyes with an occasional witty remark, but he was focused on his friends. I slipped away from the table and grabbed a barstool where I knew I'd get attention from my bartender friend Alvin, whom I'd known a lot longer than Dan. An hour went by and the bar was packed. Dan never left his booth. He may not have even noticed I was gone. After a while, I caught a glimpse of him at the far end of the bar, my friend filling his pitcher. The jukebox was blaring George Michael's "Faith" and a dance floor bloomed between barstools. I squeezed my way through the masses and tapped Dan on the shoulder.

"I think we need to talk," I said. "Can we go outside?"

"I don't want to leave my friends," he said. "But I need to tell you that I got back together with my high school girlfriend when I was home, so I don't think this is going to work."

This? You mean *us?* We're a "this?" And Dan walked off with his pitcher of beer as tears filled my eyes. The jukebox was playing "You've Lost that Lovin' Feeling." And I wanted to be gone. Gone. Gone. Whoa-ah.

Alvin came from behind the bar. "What happened?" he asked. I was only partly through my answer when he said, "That is *not* cool."

He marched over to Dan's table and told him to leave and never come back. Dan was not yet twenty-one. He only got in because he was with me.

My heart was broken, but I felt loved as Al wrapped me in a bear hug and I watched Dan walk away through the window. Alone.

CHAPTER FIFTY-ONE
Take it Or Leave it

I am sitting in the parking lot outside the dentist's office watching my mother cry. She's shaking her head at me and sobbing, obviously trying to elicit a penitent guilt that will make me change my mind.

"Dr. Brooks says you're going to California, and I just had to play along with it as if I knew all about it even though this is the first I've heard of any such crazy idea!" she sobs. "I feel like a fool! Like I don't even know my own child!"

Well, clearly you don't, I think. I look out the window feeling tears coming on. But they are not tears of culpability; they are frustrated tears. I've shared my plan, but no one was listening. No one asked any questions. No one offered suggestions. They didn't seem to believe me any more than they believed that I was going to study French in Lyon or join the Peace Corps, pipe dreams proposed repeatedly throughout college. The study abroad brochures were patently dismissed.

"Where do you think the money for *that* is going to come from?"

I chickened out on the Peace Corps after two rounds of interviews. The two-year commitment seemed like a lifetime. And Mom's initial reaction sowed fear.

"You'll get raped and likely murdered in some third world country! Is that how you want your life to end?"

But now she grits her teeth as the tears turn into anger.

"What are you going to do? You don't have any money, and don't you think that your father and I are going to support such a harebrained plan!"

A couple months before my college graduation, when my first credit card came in the mail to Morrison dorm with an $800 line of credit, my first purchase was an Eastern Airlines ticket to Los Angeles. Never mind that I'd not been further west than East Tennessee. Never mind that I had no job lined up or a plan as to where I'd live, or a car. Never mind that I'd done no research on LA and didn't know there wasn't a public transportation system like what I'd experienced in Washington, D.C. or Atlanta.

When we arrived at the dentist's office just weeks before graduation for what would be my last dental visit until I got my own insurance—which meant it was my last dental visit for several years—I was the first one called into the exam room. Dr. Brooks had been our family dentist since before my first loose tooth. With water and tools, fingers and gauze alternately in mouth, I attempted to answer his questions about my future. I shared that I'd be departing for Southern California on June 9th with a return ticket for December 22nd. I wasn't sure what I was going to do when I got there, but I was going to give myself six months to figure it out. He seemed impressed with my guts, though perhaps a bit concerned about my foolhardiness.

My mom was next in the dentist's chair and when she came into the waiting room after her checkup, she looked flustered. I figured she must have been told to come back to get some cavities filled, but when we got into the car, the tearful scene unfolded.

I wasn't backing down. The thicker her guilt trip, the more resolute I became. I knew from experience that behind that emotional brick wall was another partition of penitence soon to be constructed. I'd be shamed into taking the management track job at the department store. I'd be shamed into babysitting on Saturday nights. I'd have to make one of my sisters give up her bedroom and they'd be back to sharing a room and I'd be the awkward house guest that everyone wished would move out. I didn't have the money for an apartment yet in North Carolina. What made me think I would be able to afford a place to live in LA? Ah, but if I was destined to struggle, I wanted to do it out of sight of my mother.

I thought maybe she'd get it, having left home for a far-off place when she was even younger than me.

But she was married. I was striking out on my own.

Mom didn't go to the airport with me. She stood in the entry hallway, her face colored with ten shades of guilt. I waved goodbye with a lump in my throat as my mother wedged herself between the screen door and the front door, ostensibly so as not to let flies in the house, but also to make her point that she did not condone my departure. My father jangled the keys to the Honda, making his point that we need to stop these she-nanigans and get going or you'll miss your flight. I really only planned to be gone for six months.

And off we went, my father silent by my side. My sisters teary eyed in the backseat as I tried to talk up how much fun it would be when they visited me in California, knowing there wasn't much of a chance of my parents springing for such a trip.

I was grateful that Dad didn't ask where I was going or what I intended to do, though I probably needed to have a cogent discussion with someone before I took my $200 in savings and my Wachovia Visa with the flight I still hadn't paid off, along with my two suitcases, to a city I'd only read about in *Ramona*, seen a few times on *The Brady Bunch* and *The Beverly Hillbillies*, or heard about in Led Zeppelin and Eagles songs.

But this was my dad, and he wasn't one to ask questions. He joined the Navy at eighteen and that was the first time he'd left the Appalachian Mountains. Because my college was a rival to his favorite team, he never even crossed the literal red and blue line that spanned Highway 54 into Chapel Hill until the month before my graduation, when the family came for an Easter picnic on my campus. We were eating our tuna salad sandwiches when Daddy said, "So Suzanne, what is it you're getting your degree in anyway? Some of the fellers from work wanna know."

It wasn't that *he* was curious, it was his friends. It never dawned on either of my parents to inquire about my coursework in the four years I was there.

There are many reasons why I left. Yes, I was twenty-two and needed to find my own way. That is the story my parents heard. And yes, I was heartbroken as my little sisters clung to my legs in the jetway and I peeled their tiny fingers from the edges of my boots and kissed the tops of their golden heads, promising Christmas will be here before they know it, their pink-rimmed blue eyes looking up, pleading for me to stay. My father stood stoically and didn't intervene in the scene.

I was too emotional to be the child of a yeller. I was too questioning to be the daughter of an unquestioning Catholic. "Because I said so" is no answer, but those were my mother's favorite words.

There was a plaque hanging over the pantry in our kitchen facing my seat at the dining table: *You have two choices for dinner: Take it or Leave it.* This time, I made the choice to leave it. All of it.

Saying goodbye to my father didn't plague me. I wasn't as concerned with letting him down since he wasn't likely to let me know if I did. My sisters would soon be absorbed in their elementary school worlds and my brother was off at college, but it was my mother's opinion that haunted my heart.

CHAPTER FIFTY-TWO

The Ticket

I am standing at the gate at LAX scanning the terminal. I have just disembarked from my third airplane trip ever and I don't see the one person I know in Los Angeles. Prior to this moment, the farthest west I've ever stepped foot was the mountains of East Tennessee. Now my white cowboy boots from Payless ShoeSource are mere feet from Hollywood. Ok, miles.

The thing is, I have no idea how many miles. Truthfully, I flew to LA having never even seen a map of the city. In my defense, it is 1988. There is no internet. No MapQuest. Yes, I could have found an atlas at the library, but I'm not a particularly prepared pioneer.

I scan the terminal and don't see Mark anywhere. Mark was my resident assistant freshman year in college. We became friends, and after he graduated, we stayed in touch. We were talking a couple months earlier and he asked about my plans after graduation.

"I don't really know," I said.

"You should come out here! LA is great! You'd love it!" he said.

Fast Times at Ridgemont High and *Beverly Hills Cop* sure did make LA look great. A seed was planted. That credit card application was the water and fertilizer.

Because as the end of college neared, it was becoming increasingly clear that I'd not achieved my mother's primary goal for me in going there: the MRS degree.

"What happened with that boy you went out with last week?" Mom inquired on our regular Sunday evening calls, when telephone rates were cheapest. "Didn't you say he's going to medical school? What about that young man who's joining his family business? Is he still considering law school? When are you going to find someone and settle down?"

No one in my family seemed to care what I was getting my degree in, and now that I'd soon have a BA in Communications, the first thing I needed to communicate is that I would *not* be getting married any time soon.

So, there I am in the Eastern Airlines terminal when I realize: a ticket is not a plan. An airline ticket is not a Willy Wonka golden ticket to success.

Not seeing Mark anywhere, I head to baggage claim and wait by the carousel for my two suitcases containing all my worldly possessions meant to get me through the next six months: clothes, my Walkman with mix tapes, some books, and a manila folder with a stack of resumes.

Now I'm at the curb looking like Ellie May Clampett in my floral dress and cheap boots, standing by the faded gray bags that once belonged to my grandfather. And Mark still isn't here. I go to a phone booth and pull a folded piece of paper with his numbers on it and quarters from my purse. I call Mark's home and office and get answering machines. In the cramped booth I consider my options, watching as people who know where they're going get into cars with friends and taxis with destinations.

I'm fighting an urge to head back into the terminal to change my return ticket for the next flight back to Raleigh. What the heck was I thinking doing this? The panicked battle is raging in my mind for a full hour when Mark pulls up to the curb in his dusty red Datsun. He hops out and we hug hello.

"So sorry I'm a little late" he apologizes. "Work was insane and traffic was a nightmare."

It is the first time I have ever considered that traffic might be the reason someone is late.

"It's ok," I say brightly, though I'm near tears.

I collect myself. I am in Los Angeles, the City of Angels, and I'm ready for my next chapter!

Only really, I'm not.

Mark lives in a nondescript tan apartment building in Santa Monica. It's a bachelor pad with nothing but a bed, a couch, a coffee table, a bookshelf and a kitchenette. His monthly rent is likely twice what I spent for an entire semester in my dorm room. We make spaghetti together and eat it on the couch while watching *21 Jump Street*.

Later, after he pours us a second glass of wine, he leans over to kiss me. I move away. Ours was never a romantic relationship.

"What?" he questions. "I thought we could have some fun together."

"I-I just wasn't expecting that."

"Well, what did you expect?" He looks angry.

"This is just a little fast," I stall. But he's right, what did I expect? Did I think I was going to stay in Mark's apartment indefinitely? We hadn't really had a conversation about my plans. He said come. I bought a ticket and said I was coming. He said he'd meet me at the airport. What the heck kind of harebrained idea was this?

Mark shakes his head and walks to the bathroom. "I'm taking a shower."

He slams the door behind him. I hear the water running and wander to his bookshelf, shaking and uncertain of my next move. I'm mysteriously drawn to a plain black book amongst the Steven Kings and Robert Ludlums.

In it I find a list of women with whom Mark has had sex. Hundreds of names. He's rated them all and written descriptions of some of the acts and their locations, from awesome blowjob on a rocky cliff to doggie style in a broom closet at work. Some have names and some are people I knew in college. Others are "*blonde chick from the biker bar*" or "*black girl with the big tits.*" My name is the last one in the book with a question mark penciled in next to it.

Holy crap! What am I going to do?

I pretend to be asleep on the couch when he comes out of the bathroom. My mind races all night as I try to figure out my next steps. I am determined not to give him an answer to the question penciled into his book, so I play possum as he gets ready for work the next day. Then I grab my Walkman and head down Santa Monica Blvd until I come to the ocean. I don't know what to do, but as much as I am pulled toward home, it's clear in my first sighting of the Pacific that there is so much more for me to see and do and learn in this expansive place.

On my way back to Mark's apartment, I grab a copy of *The Los Angeles Times.*

And then I grab a cab.

"Where to?" the driver asks as he puts my suitcases into the trunk. I search my memory for what I know of Los Angeles.

"Sunset Boulevard," I say.

"That's a long road," he chuckles. I feel foolish.

"Hollywood," I declare.

Soon I'm soaking in the lush landscape of Beverly Hills then it morphs into the hard edges of the Sunset Strip and I know we can't drive like this forever. I have to call it.

"There," I say, and he lets me out at a place that it looks like I can afford. The Saharan Motel.

It's seedier than I expected. I'm not streetwise, but I can tell it wouldn't be smart to walk down Sunset with my suitcases looking for a better option. The room, with its tan shag carpet and well-worn orange floral bedspread, reeks of smoke. The sun is setting as I search the Want Ads in the *LA Times*. A professor in college had mentioned that the ad agencies he worked for were on Wilshire Blvd. I guess I'd figured I'd walk there and drop off resumes? Take the non-existent subway? Surely someone in Human Resources would see that I'd just graduated from UNC-Chapel Hill and say, "You're hired! Here's your first paycheck; get an apartment! Here's your second paycheck; get a car!"

But there aren't any advertising jobs I'm qualified for in the *LA Times*. I am still in the As, skipping over anesthesiologist, when I land on Au Pair. A place to live, a car to drive, a hundred dollars a week. I call and do a phone interview. They agree to come to Hollywood to meet me in person the next day.

I fall asleep fully clothed on top of the questionable sheets, but I am awoken abruptly by a loud banging on my door. "It's Ramona! You ready baby?!"

The peephole reveals a woman wearing leopard print and leather and leaning suggestively against the railing.

"Shit!" I grab the phone as she bangs on the door. "There's someone outside!" I whisper. She knocks even louder.

"Just ignore it," says the person at the front desk. "She'll go away."

So, I do, but about an hour later, the banging starts again. This time the voice is angry and male. I look out the peephole and there's Ramona accompanied by a large man in gold chains and a white fedora.

"When you make an appointment, mother fucker, you keep your appointment!" he yells as he slams his fist into the door. I call back downstairs. There is a commotion and then it is quiet.

I haven't slept when I meet my potential employers at the Sunset Grill. We see firsthand the working girls and basket people Don Henley sings about. Maybe the flight attendant and her pilot husband are scared for me. They hire me on the spot and I ride home with them to Palos Verdes as the new nanny to their seven-year-old daughter.

It's more than a month before I tell my mother about my new job. Back home my sisters are seven and ten. Mom isn't impressed that I traveled all this way to do something I could have done in North Carolina while making her life easier.

* * * * *

But here's the thing. There were many days when I nearly picked up the phone and changed my return ticket, but I didn't. As I shuttled my young charge around the verdant South Bay hills in the nanny's convertible under palm tree-lined streets to school and parks and playdates at the beach, I fell in love with California.

I began to see myself as a risk-taker, irrepressible, a survivor. Yet I never thought I'd stay. I was a Carolina girl, after all. My soul was rooted in Outer Banks sand and Appalachian soil. I knew the accents and the customs, the taste of sweet tea and hushpuppies, the sticky summers and crystal-covered tree limbs of a promised blizzard that amounted to little more than flurries.

But in California, I quickly embraced the Lorax-tufts of palms flapping in the breeze a mile over my head, the icy cold ocean in August, the bursting blooms of Jacaranda that dot the valley from a perch on a hike in Griffith Park.

North Carolina began to fade into my foundation, a place of the past that I could build upon, but not the land where I wanted to construct my life, though I always knew that the Cheerio trail could lead me back if ever I needed to follow it home.

After ringing in 1989 with friends in Raleigh, I came back to Los Angeles. Three decades later—after several jobs, a marriage, a couple kids, a community of friends, and a pandemic—LA continues to envelop me in her warmth. When the palm trees beckon in the breeze and the scent of jasmine fills the air, I look out over the Pacific Ocean and remember that girl who almost turned back, and I am so glad she didn't.

THE BEGINNING

Acknowledgments

My first writing teachers were my high school English teachers who were liberal with their red pens: Muriel Allison, Robert Baird and Terry Hardison. My love of writing sat on the backburner for decades, but was invigorated through the encouragement of LA-based writing teachers Bella Mahaya Carter, Robin Finn, Karin Gutman, Wendy Hammers, Terri Silverman, and Suzanne Whang. Wendy, in particular, became a dear friend, and introduced me to the sublime soul sisters in our *Kick Back & Create* and *Tasty Words* community, and gave me the encouragement to lead writing workshops, take on editing projects, and—most importantly—complete this book. We all need champions, and Wendy deserves a championship trophy.

Special thanks to Gordon McClellan, Suanne Laqueur, and Corey Stewart of DartFrog Books for their guidance, and to Tracy Kopsachilis for the beautiful cover art.

I am grateful for the people who raised me—not just my family, but the magical characters in the Old Farm neighborhood who grace the stories that have long danced in my mind and heart and have now found their way onto these pages. The Kenneys and the Lucases, in particular. Ya'll are kin.

We were fortunate to have grown up in a simpler time and lucky to be able to laugh at the foibles of our youths. My beloved mother is the foil for many of my stories, but our connection runs deep, and I miss the warmth of her smile and hugs every single day. I am so filled with gratitude toward my father, Bill Lowe, for listening without judgement and sharing his own stories with me as the years without the love of his life have turned into decades. To my brother William and my sister Marianne, you were both foundational players in my story and I am grateful for the happy memories. To my "baby" sister, Carolanne, thanks for occupying Mom's and Dad's attention when I was a teen so I could do the stupid things that make for good stories. How lucky am I to have a best friend who shares my blood?

Heartfelt appreciation to Jenny Mosley for being my first writing partner, to Pam Bassuk, Cynthia Cone, Ariel Penn and Suzanne Skrabak for our sweet and fruitful first writers' circle, and to Rachelle Elias, Pattie Fitzgerald, and Cathy Larsson for being early readers of this manuscript. I'm forever grateful to my friends at Story Salon, notably Beverly Mickens, Dan Farren, Merritt Zalon, Tony Figueroa and Donna Allen Figueroa for letting me test most of these tales on the Art Parlor stage. And a shout out to my neighbor and storytelling icon, Vicki Juditz, for opening the door to storytelling in the first place. Thanks to Lindsay Kavet for casting me in "*Expressing Motherhood*" in 2015, which led me to Ann Imig and the opportunity to produce "*Listen to Your Mother*" in Los Angeles, and to Taia Perry-Kretz for joining me on that journey. Without those experiences, I'd not have launched JAM Creative and given countless others the chance to share their stories on stage while supporting non-profits. JAM is a nod to my two favorite humans ever: my children, Jack and Maddie. You'll show up in the next book.

There are not adequate words to express my gratitude for the unwavering support of my husband, Chris. Because he is a man of few words himself, to him I offer four: hook, line and sinker.

About the Author

Born in Charleston, SC, formed in Raleigh, NC, and reborn in Southern California, Suzanne Weerts' creative nonfiction essays can be found in *The Sun* and *Good Old Days* magazines, and in several anthologies and online publications. Suzanne is a writing teacher, producer, nonprofit fundraiser and community activist who loves helping people find their voice on paper, on stage, and in standing up for meaningful causes. Her company, *JAM Creative*, has raised tens of thousands of dollars for local non-profits through storytelling events, and she can also be seen on stages across Southern California sharing her own stories including at *The MOTH*, *Story Salon*, *Revealed* and *Tales By The Sea*.

The mother of two compassionate young adults, Suzanne is mighty grateful that her mother's repeated warnings of "*Just you wait until you have children of your own!*" amounted to 98.5 percent amusement, joy and wonder. A proud graduate of the University of North Carolina at Chapel Hill, she lives in Burbank, CA with her semi-social husband and their antisocial dog. Learn more at suzanneweerts.com.

www.ingramcontent.com/pod-product-compliance
Lightning Source LLC
Chambersburg PA
CBHW031456120626
46545CB00005B/1631